THE
POCKET BOOK
OF
GOLF RULES

THE
POCKET BOOK
OF
GOLF RULES

Steve Newell

CLB

5146 The Pocket Book of Golf Rules
This edition published in 1999 by CLB
an imprint of Quadrillion Publishing Ltd., Godalming, Surrey, U.K.
Distributed in the USA by Quadrillion Publishing, Inc.
230 Fifth Avenue, New York 10001
Copyright © 1999 Quadrillion Publishing, Godalming, Surrey
ISBN 1-84100-144-9
Printed and bound in China

Photographic Credits
Phil Sheldon Golf Picture Library: 4, 6, 9, 11, 16-17, 18, 20, 23, 29, 31, 33, 35,
37, 38, 40, 43, 45, 46-47, 49, 50 top, 52, 55, 57, 59, 61, 63, 64, 67, 68,
71 right, 73, 74, 76, 79, 81, 83, 85, 86 top and bottom
All other illustrations: Quadrillion Publishing

CONTENTS

INTRODUCTION

Golf, more than any other game, is a truly self-governing pastime and thus in no other sport is there a greater onus on participants to know, understand and abide by the rules. The game is infinitely more enjoyable, not to mention fairer, if everyone plays by the same rules. It is these rules which unite golfers of all standards. The weekend player, the red-hot amateur, the struggling tour pro and the world No.1—each and every one of them must play the same game, even if the numbers at the bottom of the score card bear little resemblance.

When the first Rules of Golf were drawn up in 1744, there were only 13 in total. Today they cover hundreds of pages.

The trouble is, at golf courses around the world there are occasionally signs of a worrying lack of rule-awareness. Not through deliberate dishonesty but rather through ignorance. Regrettably few golfers are introduced to the rules of golf when they take up the game, while more experienced golfers get by on a handful of rudimentary rules, but unconsciously come to grief simply by following procedures that might seem logical, convenient and correct, but sadly are not.

Whatever the reasons, the heart of the matter is that golf is self-governing and it is therefore the golfer's duty to know the rules. While there are a good many to understand these days, a sound knowledge of the rules of golf does not require protracted study or prodigious memory. There is an enormous degree of overlap within the rules, with certain relief procedures applying to many different sets of circumstances. Providing key elements are mastered, 99 percent of every round of golf played will present very few dilemmas. Even on the rare occasion when a problem is encountered, a little lateral thinking on the part of the rule-aware golfer is usually enough to overcome the difficulty and provide an equitable solution.

Like so much in life, it used to be simpler. In 1744, when the Honourable Company of Edinburgh Golfers, officially recognized as the oldest golf club in the world, penned on one side of paper the first Rules of Golf, there were only 13 of them—and rather odd some of the rules were, too. There was no such thing as marking the ball—if an opponent's ball was in your way, you had to putt around it or find a way over it. The "stymie" was one of the many bizarre rules that was doomed to be ditched when the Royal & Ancient took over the running of the game in the mid-19th century. Since then the rule book has grown considerably, jointly presided over by the Royal & Ancient, based at St Andrews, in Scotland, the home of golf, and the USGA, based in New Jersey. Together, these two organizations efficiently govern a game that is continually changing, growing and evolving in subtle, but meaningful, ways.

The aim of the *Pocket Book of Golf Rules* is not to usurp the R&A and USGA's authority and establish a new code of conduct, but rather to support the rules while making them more understandable. The intimidating, rather dry and lifeless text so often associated with rule books is largely gone and in its place comes a more user-friendly approach—a plain-language guide to all the key rules that every golfer should know. Not only does this book bring the rules to life, it should also bring them into clearer focus. Designed to accompany the golfer on the course, it highlights key points in the clearest possible way, serving as companion and arbiter. Tucked away in the pocket of the golf bag, it can be called upon whenever required to settle contentious, possibly score-wrecking, predicaments.

Unlike the professional, the amateur golfer will not have a referee on hand to provide guidance whenever a query occurs. Being a self-governing game, the onus is on golfers to be aware of the rules to ensure that all play on the same terms. It's been that way for 250 years and it's the way ahead.

Steve Newell

IMPORTANT DEFINITIONS

The whole concept of this section may seem basic, but it's a big mistake to think you can skip by it. Much of the essential golfing terminology relating to the rules can be a little unusual, but a familiarity with these definitions will make it a lot easier to understand the rules themselves.

Addressing the ball You've officially addressed the ball when you have taken your stance and also grounded the club. So if your ball is perched precariously on tall grass, loose chippings or pine needles, it's wise to hover the clubhead at address because the ball could easily move and, if you ground the club, you will be penalized. Remember, though, you can't ground your club in a hazard, so in those situations you are deemed to have addressed the ball the moment you take your stance.

Advice There are strict rules applying to this, so it is worth knowing what it constitutes. Advice is any counsel or suggestion which could influence a player in the choice of club or the way a certain shot is played. Crucially, however, any information relating to the rules of golf or on matters such as the position of a hazard or, say, where the flag is on the green, does not count as advice.

Ball in play A golf ball is in play as soon as you've made a stroke on the teeing ground. It remains in play until you have holed out, except when it is lost, out of bounds or lifted, or another ball has been substituted under an applicable rule. You can have only one ball in play at a time. So, if your ball heads off toward a water hazard and you then drop another ball and play it, the second ball is then officially in play. Should you find your original ball and play it, whether it was in a water hazard or not, you will have played the wrong ball.

Bunker This is described as a hazard consisting of a prepared area of ground, often a hollow, from which turf or soil has been removed and replaced with sand or the like. Grass-covered ground bordering or within the bunker is not part of the bunker, so you can ground your club in those areas. The margin of a bunker extends vertically downward, but not upward.

Caddie Nice if you can get one, but here's the official line. A caddie is one who carries or handles your clubs during play and otherwise assists you in accordance with the rules.

Casual water This is defined as any temporary accumulation of water on the course which is visible before, or after, you take your stance. Obviously it doesn't count if you're up to your waist in a water hazard! Snow and ice are either casual water or a loose impediment, the choice is yours. Frost, however, is neither and does not entitle you to relief.

Committee The committee in charge of competitions is, in everyday golf clubs, unlikely to be on site at weekends. In these instances the club professional is usually authorized to act on behalf of the tournament committee.

■ *Ben Crenshaw exercises his right to choose to play out of any water hazard.*

Competitor A simple word with very subtle, but crucial, variations. A competitor is a player in a stroke play competition—so that's you in the monthly medal. A fellow competitor is the person you play with in the monthly medal or indeed any other stroke play event. Neither of you are partners and you certainly aren't playing partners. It may sound unnecessarily precise, but confusion surrounding the exact definition of the people in a group of golfers can cause problems with the rules.

Equipment This term applies to anything you use, wear or carry. Equipment also applies to your golf cart, motorized or not. The word "equipment" does not apply to the ball being played, nor to any small objects such as ball-markers, coins or tees used, say, to indicate an area in which you are about to drop a ball.

Flagstick It's what you aim for and, sadly, seldom find. Its exact description is a "movable straight indicator, with or without bunting or other material attached," which explains why it isn't a problem that some golf clubs in the US have baskets instead of flags atop the flagsticks. It must be centered in the hole, though, and it has to be circular in cross-section.

Ground under repair This is defined as any part of the course so marked by the Committee. It includes material piled for collection. It also includes any hole made by the greenskeeper, even if not so marked. The lines indicating ground under repair count as such, so if your ball is only just touching the line it counts as lying in ground under repair and you are entitled to free relief. Likewise, if you have to stand within ground under repair you are entitled to relief. It's important to note, however, that loose grass cuttings which are not obviously to be removed do not count as ground under repair.

Hazard Simple. Any bunker or water hazard. Avoid them at all costs!

The hole is required to be of specific dimensions and thus the tool required to create one is a clever piece of equipment.

Hole Easier said than found, the rules are very specific concerning the hole's size. It must be 4½ inches in diameter and at least 4 inches deep. If a lining is used, it must be sunk at least 1 inch below the surface of the putting green.

Holed Your ball is only considered holed when it is at rest within the circumference of the hole and the whole ball is below the level of the lip.

Honor A very noble term, but it simply refers to the golfer entitled to play first from the teeing ground. This can be decided on the toss of a coin on the first tee, and from thereon is determined by the player with the lowest score on the preceding hole.

Lateral water hazard This is one definition that becomes far clearer when you get to the rule itself (page 78). A lateral water hazard is one that is situated in such a way that it is not practical to drop a ball behind the hazard. You'll know when you're in one because it will be marked by red lines or stakes.

Line of play This is the direction you wish the ball to take after you've played the stroke, plus a reasonable distance on either side of the intended direction. The line of play extends vertically upward from the ground but, importantly, it does not extend beyond the hole.

Line of putt Much the same as the previous definition, only this time it applies specifically to the actual putting green. The line of a putt includes a reasonable distance either side of the intended line, but again it does not extend beyond the hole.

■ *A golfer is entitled to move any loose impediments such as leaves or branches which lie around his ball.*

Loose impediments This term applies to natural objects such as stones, leaves, twigs, branches or insects and worms. They must not be growing objects, though, and they must not be fixed or solidly embedded. If it is stuck to your ball it cannot be described as a loose impediment. One tricky issue worth bearing in mind is that sand and loose soil are loose impediments on the green, but not elsewhere.

Lost ball This is one definition that may sound blindingly obvious, but there's more to it than meets the eye. A ball is lost if it is not found or identified by you within five minutes of beginning your search. A ball is also lost if you put another ball into play under the rules, even though you might not have searched for it. Likewise if you play a provisional ball from a point where the original ball is likely to be, or from a position beyond that point, then the provisional ball is the ball in play. Your original ball is, therefore, officially lost.

Move or moved This definition is measured in fractions. If your ball leaves its position and comes to rest in any other place, it is considered to have moved. If, however, you are playing golf on an exceptionally windy day and the ball merely oscillates, that does not count as moved. Neither does it count as having moved if the face of your putter just touches the ball as you address it, provided of course it doesn't actually shift position.

Obstruction This term applies to anything artificial that could get in the way of play. It includes artificial surfaces and the sides of roads and paths. There are exceptions to this rule, though. The word obstruction does not apply to objects defining out of bounds, such as stakes, railings or a wall. So although they are definitely artificial, if your ball comes to rest against an out-of-bounds post, it's tough—you can't move the post. Also, some artificial objects can be declared an integral part of the course if the Committee of the club so decides.

Out of bounds The rules describe this as ground on which play is prohibited. When it is defined by stakes or a fence, the out of bounds line is determined by the nearest inside points of the stakes, fence or posts at ground level. But that doesn't include any angular supports. When out of bounds is determined by a white line, the line itself is out of bounds. So if your ball is on that line, you're out of bounds. You can, however, stand out of bounds to play a ball resting within bounds.

■ *The ocean is one water hazard you probably won't be retrieving your ball from.*

Outside agency This applies to any agency that is not part of the match or, in stroke play, not part of the competitor's side. It includes a referee, a marker, an observer or a forecaddie (someone who is enlisted by the committee to spot balls during play). You can't claim wind or water as an outside agency.

Partner This is a player on the same side as you in, say, a foursome, a four-ball or a better-ball match. Remember the difference—even if you are playing with your best friend in a medal, he or she is not your partner.

Penalty stroke Not something that any golfer appreciates, but it's a fact of life on the course even for the greatest players in the world. There will be plenty of situations in this book describing the instances when penalty strokes are added to your score, or your side's score. If you play this game long enough, you are bound to become quite familiar with them.

Provisional ball This is an option you take when you suspect a ball may be lost outside a water hazard, or may be out of bounds. The key things to remember are that you can play a provisional ball in either stroke play or match play, but that you cannot play a provisional ball when you suspect your ball has finished in a water hazard. Make sure you state clearly your intentions, declaring out loud that you are about to hit a provisional ball before actually doing so.

Putting green Your ball is considered to be on the putting green when any part of it actually touches the green.

Rub of the green An unusual term that refers to a situation when a ball's motion is accidentally deflected or stopped by an outside agency. It can work both for and against you. Sometimes a rub of the green will deflect a poorly struck shot on to a green it otherwise wouldn't have hit. On other occasions a decent shot can be deflected out of bounds and you will have to accept that with equal grace.

Stance Taking your stance consists of you placing your feet in position for, and preparatory to, making a stroke.

Stipulated round This consists of playing the holes of the course in their correct sequence, unless otherwise authorised by the Committee.

Stroke The fewer you make, the better. It refers to the forward momentum of the club and must involve the intention of fairly striking at, and thus moving, the ball. This is why air shots counts as strokes: you had every intention of moving the ball, but didn't. Don't forget, though, that if you manage to stop your swing halfway to the ball and before the clubhead actually reaches the ball, that doesn't count as a stroke.

Teeing ground This is where it all starts. Sometimes called a tee-box, it is a rectangular area two club-lengths in depth (it's up to you to measure that part if you want to utilize that space), the outside limits of which are defined by two tee-markers. Remember that you can stand outside the teeing ground as long as your ball is within it. You should try to make use of those two club-lengths back from the markers—the ground is frequently in better condition there simply because it is barely used by other golfers.

Through the green This is probably the single most misunderstood definition in the book. It does not apply to through the green, as in too long, but rather to the entire area of the golf course, except the tee and green of the hole being played and any hazard anywhere on the course. Don't let this one catch you out when looking up a ruling in the heat of battle.

Water hazard Different from the Lateral Water Hazard, it refers to any sea, lake, pond, river, ditch, surface drainage ditch or other open water course (whether or not it contains water), and anything of a similar nature. All ground or water within the margins of the water hazard is included as part of the water hazard. Even if you are on dry land within that hazard, don't take a practice swing that makes contact with the ground—that's a penalty. In case you are in any doubt about what type of hazard it is, water hazards are defined by yellow stakes or lines, as opposed to the red stakes or lines of a lateral water hazard. The relief procedures for the two types of water hazard do differ, and that will be dealt with later.

■ *You are allowed to play from a water hazard, but in one as narrow as this it would be extremely tricky.*

Wrong ball It's easy to play someone else's ball if you're careless when in deep rough. But believe it or not you can also play a wrong ball, owned by you, if you happen to transgress a few rules. Basically, a wrong ball is any ball other than the ball in play or a provisional ball. There is another instance in stroke play whereby if you are unsure of a certain ruling you can play two balls on the affected hole, before then clarifying the ruling after your round. Under such circumstances you are in effect playing two balls, but you are not in theory playing a "wrong" one.

ETIQUETTE

One of the most famous sporting quotes includes the memorable passage that it matters not whether you win or lose, but how you play the game. This captures the essence of etiquette and it could hardly be more accurately applied than to the game of golf.

Etiquette encapsulates a variety of elements—good behavior on the golf course, care for the golf course, personal integrity and, perhaps above all, consideration for one's playing partners and fellow competitors. The whole nature of the game as we know it depends on these codes of conduct being upheld.

Strangely, there is very little written on the subject in the official Rules of Golf—barely more than a paragraph, in fact. Etiquette comprises the largely unspoken, unwritten rules of behavior, a fact that can cause concern as there is always a real danger that new generations of golfers joining the game will be unaware of the principles. Furthermore, experienced golfers basically have no real point of reference to etiquette other than word of mouth. If they happen to be in group that is unfamiliar with these principles, then etiquette will possibly be lost on them, with serious repercussions.

If standards of etiquette are allowed to slide, then so will the player's level of enjoyment. The experience of playing on even the most picturesque course can be almost completely ruined through the thoughtlessness and inconsiderate behavior of others. Having the required equipment does not in itself make a golfer, and neither does having an elegant swing or shooting a low score. Good etiquette on the golf course is the mark of the true golfer—and of a popular one, too.

This section of the book is dedicated to outlining the key principles of etiquette and the reasons why it is so important to the whole fabric of the game of golf. It covers all the key elements a golfer should be aware of and is as important as are the Rules of Golf themselves.

Looking after the golf course

The benefits of looking after the golf course and ensuring that it is left in at least the condition in which you found it are not difficult to grasp. Regrettably, far too many golfers are either too lazy to do this, or are simply ignorant of the required "courtesies." It's important to look after the course, not just to ensure that it doesn't suffer from more wear and tear than is necessary, but also out of respect for those players who will be following you. The pitch mark you leave in the green, or the divot you leave unattended in the fairway, could spell the downfall of another player, or indeed your own on a future occasion.

Bunkers Most of us have enough trouble getting out of bunkers from a perfect lie in the sand, but when you step into a bunker and find your ball nestling in the size-10 FootJoy print of a player from an earlier group, it makes your task that much more difficult. What better motivation for not subjecting someone else to that depressing discovery. When you've finished in a bunker, use the rake provided to smooth over the footprints and the divot-mark that you leave in the sand.

Pitch marks Putting surfaces are a greenskeeper's pride and joy—no other part of the course receives such loving care and attention. Make sure you do your bit to maintain it at its best and that you don't subject the surface to the one thing that causes guaranteed long term damage—unrepaired pitch marks. Created when your ball lands on the green, these marks are completely harmless if they are repaired immediately. Left untended, though, that particular spot of the green can take weeks to recover. Pitch marks are easy to repair, either with a tee-peg or a tool designed specifically for the job and which is available in any pro shop.

Other indentations We all want perfect putting surfaces to play on, but one of the things that can destroy them is golfers leaning heavily on their putters as they wait their turn. Don't do this as it can leave a nasty mark on the green. You certainly wouldn't want your birdie putt veering off line at the last minute due to someone else's carelessness, so don't risk doing it to others.

■ *Leaning on your putter can leave an indentation on the green which could deflect a ball from its natural course.*

Flagstick Even if you are feeling a little unhappy with your play, don't take it out on the flagstick or the green. When you remove the flagstick, place it gently on the ground, don't launch it javelin-style across the green.

Divots Good and bad shots alike can shift huge divots. Whether you're happy or ashamed of the shot that left its mark on the fairway, make sure you cover it up by replacing the divot. Just as unattended pitch marks cause long-term damage to the greens, so unreplaced divots can ruin a fairway, not to mention make it look very unattractive. Give it a good stamp into the ground to make sure it's securely in place before you set off toward the green.

Fill in divots on par-3s Soil-and-seed mixtures are often placed by the tee-markers on par-3s and this is considered the desired repair job, rather than replacing the actual divot you've just taken. This is not simply because the teeing ground will benefit in the long run, but because loose divots can offer a pretty insecure footing for following golfers.

Mark your ball Before you putt out take a moment to assess whether in doing so you will have to tread on your playing partner's or fellow competitor's line to the hole. Footprints in themselves create no long-term damage, but they can leave indentations that last long enough to knock another ball off its natural line. If you are in any doubt, mark your ball with a small coin or a ball-marker and wait to putt out.

Respect for fellow competitors

The pleasure to be had from playing a round of golf can so easily turn sour through the rude or inconsiderate behavior of others. Here is the indispensable guide to becoming a considerate golfer.

Dress code If you're visiting a course for the first time, it's always wise to check the dress codes both inside the clubhouse and out. Jeans and T-shirts are not permitted at the majority of golf clubs. Training shoes are frequently frowned upon too, as are short socks worn with shorts. Some clubs will insist on a jacket and tie for lunch in the dining room, even on a very hot day, which can get visiting golfers literally hot under the collar.

Timekeeper Try to arrive on time for the games you've arranged. It may sound trivial, but some people find it quite stressful and certainly very off-putting if the last few minutes prior to teeing off in a competition are spent fretting about whether the final member, or indeed any other member, of the group is actually going to turn up. You may not mind being a last-minute arrival, but try to make it to the tee in good time and remember that others could be unsettled by an anxious wait.

Waiting your turn Stand in the correct position when you are waiting to tee off so as not to provide a distraction to the others playing in your group. It is generally felt that the best place to stand is to the right and in front of the player teeing off, basically at an angle of 45 degrees to the target line. Stand still, too, because it's amazing how movement can catch the corner of the eye and put players off their stroke.

Watch out Don't make practice swings in view of your fellow competitors or playing partners as they play or prepare to hit a shot—it's bound to distract them. Also, be careful where you make a practice swing—the clubhead can travel at speeds in excess of 100mph and golfers have been injured, even killed, through careless practice swings.

Look out Keep an eye on the shots played by the golfers in your group, especially off the tee. If it looks as though it might hit someone, shout Fore!...loudly. And if you hit a shot into deep rough, even trees, try to mark the "point of entry" with a distinguishing feature—something that will help

■ *Lend a hand if those in your group lose a ball. You'd want them to do the same for you.*

you walk straight to the ball. Show some enthusiasm when helping your fellow competitors look for their ball—it's inconsiderate not to do so and also helps avoid slow play.

Pace of play A game of golf isn't supposed to be a race, but it isn't meant to be played at a crawl, either. Just as a slow driver can cause traffic jams, so it only takes one slow group of golfers to cause a backlog on the entire course. Make no mistake, slow play can be just as infuriating as any traffic jams. So it's important you make sure you know how to keep the pace of play moving along smoothly. It's very straightforward if you just remember a few guidelines.

Do call through the group behind if you can't find your ball immediately. Although the Rules of Golf allow you to look for a ball for five minutes, if you can't find your original ball immediately, the correct procedure is to wave the group behind to come through, provided of course they are ready to play. Ideally, you should also have played a provisional off the tee if you suspected your ball might be tough to find. That then saves you the additional delay of having to walk back to play three off the tee. It's amazing how these little delays add up.

Don't hit unless you are sure the group ahead is out of range. You may be in a hurry, you may think the group in front is playing slowly, you may even be feeling impatient, but hitting a potentially lethal object 250 yards through the air into the vicinity of the players in front is to be avoided. What may be your idea of a subtle reminder to the group in front to get a move on could easily have nasty consequences.

Do leave your golf bag on the correct side of the green, so that you can pick it up on the way past to the next tee. It doesn't take a lot of thought, and again it's amazing how those few saved seconds can add up over 18 holes.

Don't mark your card on the green of the hole you've just played—this is particularly annoying for those waiting to hit their approach shots. It must have happened to you, so don't put others through the same agony. Mark your card on the way to the next tee, or on the next tee if it isn't your honor.

Do keep an eye on the group in front. If they stretch out a gap of say one hole, make every effort to catch up.

Do make sure you are ready to play when it's your turn. If it's an approach shot to a green, make your club selection calculations and practice swings while your playing partner or fellow competitors are hitting their shots. As long as you're not in their line of sight, you won't put them off. On the green, you can easily find a few seconds to read the line of a putt while others are themselves preparing to putt.

Finally, remember it isn't about whether you win or lose but how you play the game, so always smile and shake hands afterward. It doesn't take a lot of effort!

THE RULES OF PLAY

The game itself

Golf has always consisted of playing a ball from the teeing ground into the hole by a stroke, or successive strokes, in accordance with the rules of the game. It sounds a simple enough pursuit and certainly the definition gives few clues as to the challenges, which are among the attractions of the game. Another appealing aspect is the number of different formats in which the game can be played. For everyday play, there are two main formats.

Match play This is thought to have been the original form of golf and is, in fact, the main format of play at some of the older-established clubs.

The terms of engagement are straightforward enough. The game is played by holes. A hole is won by the side, or player, that takes the fewest strokes on each given hole. So if you win the first hole, you are then what is described as "one up." If you lose the first hole, you are "one down" and if you halve it, in other words take the same number of shots as your opponent, you are "all square." Each subsequent hole is played on the same basis, the score being kept on a cumulative basis.

The outcome of the game is decided when you are either "up" or "down" by more holes than there are left to play. So, for instance, in a match played over one round, if you reach a situation where you are "four up" with only three holes to play you are deemed to have won the match by the margin of 4&3. Conversely, say you lose the 17th to go two down with only the final hole to play, you are the loser, this time by a margin of 2&1.

Dormie is a term used to describe a situation where you or your opponent are "down" by the same number of holes that are left to play. So let's say you are having a good day and you've just won the 15th to go 'three up', your opponent is thus "dormie-three down." If your opponent then wins the final three holes to square the match, a sudden-death playoff on extra holes usually decides the outcome.

The onus is on you to ensure that your scores are correct before you hand in your card.

One of the nuances of match play that separates it from other forms of play is the "concession," whereby your opponent is allowed to concede you a putt from short range. Equally, if you are feeling generous, you too can concede putts to your opponent. It's a charming aspect of the game and, as well as saving time, has an element of gamesmanship to it. For instance, early in a round, when there's no pressure, you may decide to concede your opponent a two footer, perhaps lulling him into the feeling that all putts of that length will be conceded. Then, later in the round, you can surprise him by making him hole an 18-inch putt, when the pressure is on. Of course, you may have the same done to you, but that's one of the many "attractions" of match play.

Stroke play This form of golf now dominates competitive play at clubs around the world. It's all about you, your clubs, a pencil and a score card. It's the format the professionals play by on tour 99 percent of the time and it's the format you will face in club medals.

The principle couldn't be simpler. Each competitor compiles a score and the winner is the one with the lowest total. The outcome is based either on the net score—in other words total number of strokes minus the player's handicap—or gross score, where no handicaps are taken into account. The latter is the way the pros play, obviously, and that's how leading tournaments such as club championship are decided in the amateur game.

Unlike match play, no one can grant you a concession in stroke play, so don't expect compassion from your playing partner when you rattle a putt three feet past the hole and don't like the prospect of the putt coming back. He can't help you. Nobody can. You're on your own and, like it or not, you have to hole out on every green.

OTHER FORMS OF PLAY

Whereas most pursuits exist in one particular format, golf is completely the opposite. There are dozens of different ways to keep score and compete against an opponent, each fascinating in its own way. Some of these games will actually form the basis of official competitions at certain clubs. Others are really only to be enjoyed among a group of friends. Whatever the reason, all the variations are worth a try.

Foursomes A popular game at many clubs, this format involves two teams of two playing against one another over 18 holes. Much quicker than the everyday game, it is often played in winter, when a brisk pace of play is desirable.

Each pair plays the same ball, with one partner teeing off on the odd-numbered holes and the other partner teeing off on the even-numbered holes. Once the tee shots are hit, the pair play alternate shots until the ball is either in the hole or conceded by the opponents. Because each player knows that it is their partner's responsibility to play the next shot, foursomes involves a strong element of teamwork and camaraderie. There is also a certain amount of strategy involved in deciding who tees off at the odds or evens.

The longer hitter of the two is obviously best utilized on the long holes, so a team would try to avoid having him or her hit too many tee shots on par-3s. Likewise, an accurate, but short, hitter doesn't want to be on the tee on the longest holes on the course. Neither would you want a great pitcher of the ball playing too many tee shots on short par-4s, when his strengths lie in hitting accurate approach shots.

Shots are given or received on the basis of three-eighths of the difference of the combined handicaps of each pair. So, for instance, if team A has a combined handicap of 23 and team B has a combined handicap of 7, then team A will receive six shots over 18 holes (in other words, three-eighths of the combined difference of 16).

Stableford This is a popular form of scoring at golf clubs around the world and can be applied to a variety of different playing formats—singles, four-ball better-ball, foursomes, greensomes—almost any game in fact. The key factor is that it's a pencil-and-score-card system, although very different from normal medal play.

Basically, the number of shots you take on each hole earns a certain number of points. A par is worth two points, a bogey is one point, a birdie three points, an eagle four points and that rarest of birds, an albatross, five points. If you can't score better than a bogey you pick your ball up and score no points for that hole. You then add up all of these points at the end of the round and the highest score wins.

Naturally, handicaps come into play in most stableford competitions and that means that your net score is the one that counts. The number of strokes received is usually calculated on three-quarters of your full handicap. So if you play off a handicap of 16, you will receive a stroke on every hole with a stroke index on the card of 12 and under. So on stroke index number five, your par is effectively a birdie, your bogey effectively a par, and so on. It's a great format, not least because your total disaster holes count no worse than a double-bogey—on a par-4 you can take 10 shots or seven, the result is still the same.

Greensomes This is a more forgiving, and frequently played, variation of foursomes. It involves a partnership hitting alternate shots with the same ball, but only after both players have teed off and chosen the best drive. There's no decision-making required on the odds and evens. Both players drive off and then decide on the most favorably positioned of the two lies from which to play alternate shots.

Greensomes is really popular at society and guest invitation days and has almost replaced foursomes at these events. For one thing, it feels more of a complete round because both players get to tee off on every one of the 18 holes—and if you are only playing that particular course, say, once a year then that's obviously desirable. Also, it's not as mentally demanding as foursomes. Each pairing has at least two opportunities to get a good tee shot away on each hole, whereas with foursomes that responsibility falls to one player.

Yellowsomes This is a cruel variation of greensomes and, make no mistake, there is potential here for disaster on a grand scale. It must be said, though, that it can be great fun when played in the right company. The concept is identical to greensomes. Played on a two-against-two basis, both golfers in each pairing tee off on every hole, then hit alternate shots from then on. The difference is that instead of each pair selecting their best tee shot, as with greensomes, in yellowsomes it is the opponents who get to pick the worst tee shot of the two. If you and your partner both hit the fairway, count your blessings because you are guaranteed a shot from the short grass. If you hit a great drive, though, and your partner doesn't, well...you're not going to like your next shot, that's for sure. There's even more pressure in this game than in regular foursomes, because the last thing you want to do is land your partner in trouble after he's just nailed one down the middle of the fairway.

Texas Scramble This is another popular format on guest invitation days. Texas Scramble can be played in teams of two, three or four, although the principle remains the same irrespective of the number of players in each team. Each member of the team tees off and they then decide on the best drive. Every member of the team then hits a second shot from that spot. The best-placed second shot is then chosen and again every member of the team plays a third shot from that spot. So every member of the team has a go at the same drive, the same second shot, the same putt and so on until someone holes out. As you can imagine it is possible to shoot some amazingly low scores—in a group of useful amateurs an under-par score in the teens is quite commonplace. It's a huge thrill to be racking-up birdies like never before, and from a social standpoint it's an unbeatable format because players in a team hardly ever leave each other's side. If there is a downside to Texas Scramble it is that it can take rather a long time to get around the 18 holes.

American Stableford This is often known by the numerical tag "6-3-0" and that provides a strong clue as to the nature of this scoring format.

It's the perfect game when you are in a three-ball, either out of choice or perhaps due to the fourth member of a four-ball group oversleeping! There are a possible nine points up for grabs on every hole. Six points for the player who wins the hole outright, three for the player who secures second place, and no points for the player who finishes last. Points are accumulated on this basis through the course of the round. If there's a two-way tie for the lowest score on a particular hole, the points are distributed 3-3-0. If there's a three-way tie then obviously the score remains unchanged. The player with the highest number of points after 18 holes is the winner. The handicap allowance is identical to regular match play: three-quarters of the difference.

Cross Country A rare game these days, as greenskeepers become increasingly sensitive to the damaging effect it can have on the course.

The name gives away the nature of the game, really. The self-appointed architects of the tournament literally throw away the score card and come up with a series of "new" one-off holes, usually nine, that bear absolutely no resemblance to the existing pattern of holes on the course. So you might play from the 1st tee to the 5th green, or from the 9th tee to the 8th green, or whatever other bizarre creation happens to come to the new course architect's mind. It's challenging, interesting and, above all, great fun.

THE TOOLS OF THE TRADE

Much deliberation goes into choosing golf equipment, and rightly so, because it isn't cheap. But do you know what you are and are not allowed to carry in your golf bag? You should, because ignorance is no excuse if you break the rules.

Rule 4   Clubs

There was a time when there was no limit to the number of clubs you were allowed to carry on to the golf course. While caddies may not have relished the prospect of bearing such a burden, the players would surely have delighted at the freedom of choice. No limit on numbers meant a profusion of specialist, or "utility" clubs, with hardly a situation that a player couldn't prepare for in the shape of a club designed specifically for the job.

All good things come to an end, though, and the authorities eventually decided that the situation needed regulating. In the 1930s a limit of 14 clubs was imposed by the governing bodies of golf and the figure has remained at this level ever since.

The rules relating to clubs, however, are broader than simply limiting the number of "sticks" a golfer can carry.

If you break a club There are many ways of breaking a club, apart from in anger. If you break a club in the normal course of play, then you are perfectly entitled to replace it with another, providing you can do so without delaying play. If, however, you do break a club in anger, that's tough. You can't replace it, you just have to live with it and hope it isn't a crucial one, such as a putter or driver.

If you want to add to your set This, in some ways, is one of the most lenient rules in the book. If you are in the middle of a round and you decide, for whatever reason, that you want to add a club to your existing set, then you are perfectly entitled to do so. Again, it's on the proviso that you don't hold up play and, of course, providing you don't already have 14 clubs in your bag.

■ *Equipment has come a long way since the old days of hickory shafts and pencil-thin golf bags (opposite).*

If you carry too many clubs

This breach of the rule book can have serious consequences, but the penalty depends on whether you are involved in a match play or stroke play event.

If it's match play, the penalty depends how far you are into the game, because you basically have to deduct one hole for every hole you've carried the extra baggage, up to a maximum of two holes.

So if you've played four holes and suddenly come across a 15th club in your bag, you are two down before you've even taken into account the actual match score.

In a stroke play event, you are penalized two strokes for each hole played with that extra "baggage," this time up to a maximum of four strokes. That's just as costly as the match play penalty, because if you don't discover your mistake until the third, you have to add four strokes to your score at the end of the round. That's like playing one more hole than everyone else—costly!

Incidentally, it doesn't matter if you are carrying one extra club or five, the penalty is the same. Somewhat surprisingly, you can also share clubs, provided the total number of clubs shared between you is no more than 14.

Rule 5 The ball

You may take the ball for granted, but that little white thing is a complicated piece of equipment. For a start, its dimensions and performance characteristics are rigidly monitored by the game's governing bodies. The ball must not be designed, manufactured or intentionally modified to have flight properties different from those of a symmetrically spherical ball. It must be not less than 1.68 inches in diameter, although there are larger golf balls on the market, and it must not weigh more than 1.62 ounces. Nor should its initial velocity be permitted to exceed 250 feet per second. And, just so you know, no foreign material may be applied to the ball for the purposes of changing its playing characteristics.

Damaged goods The rules are very specific about what constitutes "damage" on a golf ball and the appropriate procedures must be followed to the letter. Basically, a ball is described as "unfit for play" when it is visibly cut, cracked or out of shape. If you have reason to believe that your ball is damaged in some way—perhaps you have just thinned an iron shot and think it might have put a "smile" on the ball—then you are entitled to pick it up to inspect it. However, you must first notify your fellow competitors of your intentions and, in the presence of a witness, mark its position with, say, a tee-peg or coin. Now you can pick it up and it is up to your fellow competitor to verify the decision. If there is a consensus that the ball is indeed damaged, then you can go ahead and replace it before you play your next shot.

The procedure is the key here. You must call over your fellow competitor before you even touch the ball. Failure to comply with this "ID Protocol" carries a one-shot penalty in a stroke play event and an immediate loss of hole in match play.

Breaking-up is hard to do It isn't likely to happen very often, but let's just say the ball you are playing does break into pieces at the moment of impact. It will certainly come as a bit of a shock, but what happens next? Well, the rules are naturally sympathetic. It's clearly not your fault, so before you compose your letter of complaint to the manufacturer, simply cancel that stroke and play another ball from the same spot. There's no penalty involved.

Personal ID

As anyone who has ever been in a golf shop will have noticed, there are an awful lot of different balls on the market. On top of that, golf balls are numbered from one to eight. Together then, this creates a series of permutations that run into the thousands. Surely, therefore, you are unlikely to confuse two golf balls on the course? Don't you

■ *Golf balls used to be stitched leather stuffed with feathers, today they are made of complex rubber compounds.*

believe it. Identical golf balls can come into close contact on the course and that's a recipe not only for confusion, but disaster. This is why it is always wise to personalize your golf balls. It's easy enough to do by simply making a "mark" of your own, such as a pattern of dots or a squiggle around the maker's name, with a permanent marker.

If you consider this unnecessary, think again. Virtually every tour pro does it. There is a documented incident in a club competition of two golfers each looking for their golf ball in the same patch of rough. They found both balls, sitting virtually side by side. But the manufacturer's name was the same...and so was the number. Of course, neither golfer could identify which ball was his. So what was the ruling? Both were deemed "lost balls." Learning the Rules of Golf can sometimes be a painful experience.

Rule 6 The player

You may think that trying to put together a good competition round is more than enough to worry about on the course, but alas there are other responsibilities that fall on your shoulders. To be honest, they're not especially onerous, but if you're not clued-in it is easy to miss something and end up paying the penalty.

Handicap It's up to you to know your playing handicap. In match play, it is this information that determines the strokes given or received. If you start a match having declared an incorrect handicap, even if by mistake, this obviously affects the number of strokes given and you are disqualified.

The penalty is equally harsh if you make the same mistake in a stroke play event. It's up to you to know your handicap and to record this information on the score card before you sign and return it. If you fail to do so, or you enter the wrong handicap, which naturally affects the number of strokes you receive, then you are disqualified from the competition.

Be punctual Starting times in competitions are there for a reason and you have to adhere to them or face disqualification. There is, however, the merest hint of leniency with this rule. If you arrive at the first tee within five minutes of your allotted starting time and are ready and able to tee off, then the committee may waive the penalty of disqualification and simply impose a two-shot penalty in stroke play or loss of the first hole in match play. Don't bank on this, though, as you must have a very good excuse. Also, any reprieve assumes you can find a member of the committee there and then (unlikely!) or the club pro or secretary of the club, who fulfil the same role in the absence of a committee member.

Learn to keep count Within this ruling lurks another potential nightmare, because submitting a score card with an incorrect score on a hole is a no-win situation. If your card records a score on any hole that is higher than the number of strokes you actually took, then that higher score stands. If, on the other hand, your score card states a score on any hole that is lower than the number of strokes you took, then you are disqualified.

This may seem harsh bearing in mind that it is your fellow competitor, not you, who marks your card. The onus, however, is on you to check it thoroughly before you sign it. Don't take anything for granted. You only have to look back to the 1968 US Masters for a heartbreaking example of this very strict rule. Roberto de Vicenzo completed his final round level with Bob Goalby and was no doubt mentally prepared to compete in the playoff that would decide the championship. To his horror, however, minutes later he discovered that his playing partner had marked him down for a four on the penultimate hole instead of the three he had actually taken. De Vicenzo hadn't spotted the mistake, had thus signed his card and the higher score counted. This meant that he was one stroke behind and Bob Goalby was declared the winner.

Looking on the bright side, especially for the mathematically challenged, no one is penalized for incorrect addition. If the individual scores for each hole are entered correctly, but you add them up incorrectly, you are in the clear because it's up to the committee to ensure that all the numbers add up.

Stop and go A round of golf on the professional tour has become a painfully slow experience, sometimes as long as four-and-a-half hours for a three-ball. But perhaps the most worrying aspect of this is that "slow-play syndrome" appears to have spread to the amateur game. Don't succumb to the snail's pace. It makes life miserable for everyone and you may one day get penalized for it. Indeed, it's a two-stroke penalty in stroke play and the loss of a hole in match play if you continually hold up play. If you then don't get a move on you may even be disqualified altogether.

Yes, torrential rain is incredibly unpleasant, makes your grips slip and your feet sodden. But **no**, you can't use it as an excuse to stop playing. **Yes**, if the course becomes unplayable through flooding you can then stop and **yes**, lightning is a good enough excuse—the rules do allow you to stop if you feel you are in danger.

Rule 7 Practice

There are obviously no rules of golf applicable when you're at the driving range or hitting balls on the practice green—apart from the various safety considerations, of course—so this particular aspect of the rule book outlines to what extent you are permitted to practice on the course during a competitive round. It is a delicate subject and you need to be absolutely clear on it and adhere religiously to the correct procedures.

Let's first deal with stroke play, the strictest of the two formats. Most crucially of all, you are not allowed to practice on the golf course before your round. Neither can you practice on the course between rounds in a 36-hole competition, even if the rounds are to be played on consecutive days. This means that from the moment you finish your first round on Saturday lunch time, say, you can't decide to go out on the course to hit a few balls prior to your second round on Sunday. If you are caught doing this—even if it's something as apparently harmless as hitting a putt on one of the greens—you will be disqualified.

In match play, however, you can practice on the golf course before your round. Once you are on the course, either in match play or stroke play, the rules do allow you some leeway on practicing. For instance, after holing out on a green, you are allowed to practice putt or chip on or around the green of the hole you have just finished playing. You cannot hit a practice shot out of a hazard, though, such as a bunker. Neither can you practice on the green if it means that you unduly delay play—remember, a golfer who unduly delays play is himself subject to penalty. The penalty for any breach of this rule is two strokes in a stroke play event and the loss of hole in match play. An interesting point here is that the loss of hole in match play applies to the next hole, rather than

> If you are involved in some sort of delay on the tee, you are allowed to play a few innocuous chip shots near or even on the tee of the hole you are waiting to play. The rules relating to practice on the course will not penalize you for doing so, providing you do not unduly delay play.

You can do pretty much what you like on the practice green, but on the golf course the rules relating to practice are very strict.

the hole you've just played. So if one of you in a match breaches the rule by playing out of a bunker, say on the 5th green after you've both holed out, you can basically skip the 6th hole because the offender will have forfeited that hole without even getting to the tee.

Don't take practicing on the golf course lightly. Even casually knocking a stray ball back on to the range can land you in trouble if it is felt that in doing so you might have been working on, say, the rhythm of your swing. It sounds ridiculous, but you can get pulled-up in an instant on any one of these points, so it really is important you think before you act. Just one moment of impetuosity can cost you very dearly.

Rule 8 Advice

Remember, advice is any counsel or suggestion which could influence a player in determining his play, the choice of club, or the method of making a stroke. Basically, this means that you can ask on matters that are described as "public information," such as what distance it is from, say, a certain tree or fixed sprinkler head to the front of the green. The key point is that these are permanent objects. However, you can't ask that same person what the distance is from your golf ball to the front of the green. It may seem like splitting hairs, but it's important you understand this subtle distinction, because Murphy's Law states that the one time you do phrase the question incorrectly it will be directed at the canny rules expert who is always looking for a sniff of an advantage—no matter how seemingly unfair.

There are many other examples of the nuances of what constitutes advice and what doesn't. It pays to make a mental note of them.

You **cannot** ask your opponent or fellow competitor what club they have just hit.

You **can**, however, peer into his golf bag to see the number on the club. If, understandably, he doesn't want you to know and covers his clubs with a towel, for instance, you **cannot** fling the towel away to catch a sneaky glimpse.

You **cannot** give technical advice to your opponent or fellow competitor. OK, so you probably won't want to tell an opponent where he's going wrong at the top of his backswing, but even if you're five-up and suddenly overcome by goodwill you must resist the temptation because it is you who will be penalized for giving the advice in this instance. Your opponent cannot be penalized for hearing something and will be delighted to win a hole back unexpectedly. If in doubt, say nothing!

Indicating the line of play You will recall the definition relating to "line of play." It is the *direction that the player wishes his ball to take, plus a reasonable distance either side of that line.* You need to be careful about this line of play, especially when you are on the green. It is a sensitive area.

When you are preparing to putt, the line of play may be pointed out to you, say by your caddie, but in doing so the line of play must not be touched and the caddie must move away before you begin your stroke. Neither can a mark be put down to indicate the line for putting.

Away from the putting green things become a little more relaxed. Basically, if you can't see what you're aiming at, anyone can help you by indicating the line to the target. However, that person must move before you play the stroke, which they may wish to do anyway in the interests of safety! But if it is a particularly brave individual, or a very loyal friend, just make sure they move in the interests of your score! It's a two-stroke penalty for that breach of the rules, or loss of hole in match play.

■ If a ball comes to rest on a pop-up sprinkler head, you are entitled to move your ball away from the obstruction.

Information   Rule 9

All parties involved in a match should be aware of the number of strokes taken, including any penalty strokes incurred along the way. So if you incur a penalty you have to inform either your fellow competitor or your opponent as soon as is practicable. Failure to do so is like being asked how many you took on a given hole and coming up with the wrong answer—and that's cheating! Bear in mind that you don't have to state the obvious. If you are playing a par-3 over water and your tee shot plummets into the drink 50 yards short of the green, words are neither necessary nor desirable—from either party!

ORDER OF PLAY

*It would be mayhem on the golf course, with balls flying from all
directions, if there was no distinct rule governing the actual order of
play. Imagine it, in a group of four it would be hard to figure out what
on earth was going on.*

Rule 10 The order of play

Here are the order of play procedures that help keep things running
smoothly from the first tee to the final green.

On the tee The side entitled to tee off first is said to have the "honour."
This is decided on the first tee either by the order of the starting sheet, or in
match play by whichever name is highest on the draw sheet. In the absence
of this information it can simply be decided on the toss of a coin.

Thereafter it could not be simpler. The
golfer with the lowest score on each hole
takes the honor on the next tee. It is
decided on the gross score in a stroke
play event and on the net score in a
match play competition. If a hole is
halved, then the honor is simply retained
by the golfer who teed-off first on the
previous hole.

Losing order Strictly speaking,
playing out of turn off the tee in a stroke
play event carries no penalty. But you
shouldn't make a habit of it. For one thing
it could really aggravate your fellow
competitors. Worse still, if a committee
decides that an unfair advantage is being
sought in doing so—for all they know
competitors may have cooked up some

> If you need to play a provisional ball or a second ball from the tee, you should do so after your opponent or fellow competitors have hit their first tee shots. Besides, it's good to gather your thoughts after a destructive shot rather than rush in impulsively and hit another ball.

mutual arrangement—then those golfers can be disqualified from the competition.

It's different in match play. If you tee off when it isn't your turn, your opponent is entitled to cancel that shot and ask you to play it again. Obviously he or she wouldn't exercise that option if you had just knocked your ball into a fairway bunker—the opponent is equally entitled to let the shot stand—but if you've just hit your finest drive down the middle of the fairway you may, in some company, find yourself re-teeing a second ball. And you won't relish that prospect.

Elsewhere on the course Once you're off the tee, the order of play is determined by distance from the flag and it is the golfer furthest from the hole who is entitled to play first. There is no penalty for playing out of order in stroke play, but in match play an opponent can cancel the stroke and request that it be played again.

Putting out The green is the one area of the course where the order of play is not necessarily determined by who is furthest from the hole. First putts are usually determined by that, but when the balls get closer to the hole, the order of play can change. For instance, in stroke play you can carry on putting until the ball is in the hole, although it is good etiquette to ensure that you don't trample all over someone else's line to the hole. In match play, however, you do not have that right. You can, of course, ask your opponent if you can hole out, but your request will almost certainly be declined.

Measuring distance On the green it can often be difficult to tell whose ball is furthest from the hole and thus who should putt first. This is where you need to do a bit of measuring, either with the flagstick or by pacing it out. If by accident you move the ball in the process of measuring distance, there is no penalty. You simply replace it on its original spot.

THE TEEING GROUND

This is where it all starts—possibly the beginning of a new round and, at the very least, the beginning of a new hole. Make no mistake, a good start comes down to more than simply producing a fine golf swing.

Rule 11 Teeing ground

The teeing ground, or tee-box, is a rectangular area two club-lengths deep bordered either side by two tee-markers. You cannot move either of the two tee-markers, but you can stand outside them provided the ball is teed between them. There are more benefits to this than you might imagine. Utilizing the full width of the teeing ground can improve your "angle of

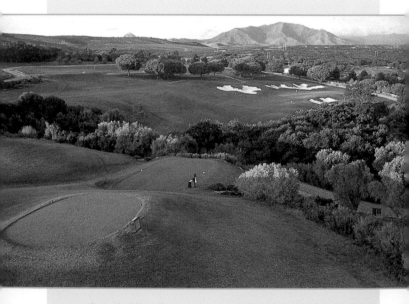

■ *Utilizing the full width of a teeing area can give you a better line into the flag on a par-3 hole.*

attack" on certain holes, so it may help you to aim away from trouble on a par-4, or perhaps give you a more direct line into a cunningly positioned flag on a par-3. Using the full two club-lengths depth of the teeing ground can also prove beneficial, particularly in winter, when the further back you go the less worn the turf is likely to be. That's sure to help you play a better shot.

> 66 Ignore the smart aleck who says "one." That accidental nudge does not constitute one shot—you simply replace the ball on the tee and start again. 99

Here are a few reminders to make sure you don't incur penalties on the teeing ground.

False start First, we dispel a myth. If at address you nudge the ball off its tee-peg with your clubhead, ignore the smart-aleck who says "one." For a start, that accidental nudge does not constitute one shot—you simply

replace the ball on the tee and start again. And secondly, it's a feeble attempt at humor, so don't even feel you need to offer a reply.

Out of place If you have something of a mental block and play a shot from outside the teeing ground, the rules vary according to the format of the game you're playing and, to a certain degree, the benevolence of your opponent. In match play your opponent has every right to ask you to play the shot again, admittedly without penalty, but if you've just smashed your ball straight down the middle it will feel like a "mental penalty" if you are then forced to replay the shot. In stroke play the procedures are more clear cut. You incur a penalty of two strokes and then have to play a ball from between the tee-markers. This is called "three off the tee."

Incidentally, even if you mistakenly play from the back tee, when there is obviously no advantage gained because you are effectively playing a longer hole than everyone else, you are still in breach of the rules and the procedures outlined above therefore apply.

PLAYING THE BALL

This is the whole essence of the game—hitting that little white, spherical object. Not only is it a complicated process from a physical standpoint, but there are also some intriguing rules to bear in mind.

Rule 12 Searching for and identifying your ball

There is a two-step procedure involved here. First, you've got to search for your ball. Then, only when you find it, can you begin to identify it. Obviously if you are in the middle of the fairway there is no searching required and there will be no problems in identifying your ball. This part of the rule book deals predominantly with areas of the course where it perhaps isn't obvious where your ball is or, indeed, whether it's your ball or not.

In long grass You are allowed to touch or bend long grass, rushes, bushes, heather and the like, but only to the extent necessary to find and identify your ball. You need to be delicate here—don't go rummaging around like a maniac—and in the process you must not improve the lie of the ball, the area of your intended swing, or the line of play. If the lie is really appalling, the rules do permit you to lift the ball for the purposes of identifying it. You can't do this in a hazard, though, and you certainly can't use the exercise as an excuse to improve your lie, either. It's also very important that before you even touch the ball you first announce your intentions to your opponent or fellow competitor. Then, in the presence of a witness, you can mark the position of the ball, pick it up, identify it (cleaning away excess dirt, but only if absolutely necessary) and replace it in the exact position it was in before being lifted. If you don't follow this procedure to the letter, you will be penalized one stroke.

In a bunker If your ball is completely buried in a bunker, which can happen in certain types of sand, you are allowed to brush aside as much sand as is necessary to confirm that the ball is there. But that's as far as you can go. You don't actually need to identify it as your ball, because there is no penalty for playing a wrong ball in a hazard. If the ball moves while you are brushing aside the sand, or if you brush aside too much sand and thus effectively improve the lie, do not panic—there is no penalty. However, you must restore the lie to its original state. It's a two-stroke penalty for a breach of this rule, or loss of hole in match play.

Fishing for your ball can be a depressing experience—don't make it worse by not following the correct procedure thereafter.

In a water hazard Identifying a ball in a water hazard? No, we're not talking about a full scuba-diving expedition into the lake on the 15th fairway. This is a shallow-water exercise. Basically if you think you can see your ball, or the water is so murky that you think it's there but you're not quite sure, you are allowed to probe around for it with a club. The ball will almost certainly move if your club comes across it, which obviously isn't a problem if all you are then going to do is fish it out and drop under penalty. But if you decide you want to have a go at playing out of the water hazard, a risky option by any standards, you must attempt to nudge the ball back to its original position in the water hazard before you play the stroke. Tricky and, to be honest, not recommended.

In casual water or ground under repair It would be easy for the ball to move in the process of you trying to identify it in, say, some quite deep casual water, abnormal ground condition, or ground under repair. There is no penalty for this occurring, but if you intend playing the ball from the condition in which is it lying, you must first replace it on its original spot. If, on the other hand, you intend to take relief, you simply pick it up and proceed accordingly. Once again, the penalty is two strokes or loss of hole in match play for breaking this rule or for any of the above-mentioned misdemeanors in a water hazard.

Rule 13

Ball played as it lies; lie of the ball, area of intended swing and line of play; stance

The heading alone for this section appears daunting, but don't worry, it's not actually as complicated as it sounds. Let's break it down as much as possible to make it more easily digestible.

You **must** play the ball as it lies. It's one of the oldest rules in golf, going right back to the 18th century, and should be obeyed except as otherwise provided in the rules.

You **can't** improve the position or lie of your ball, the area of your intended swing, your line of play or a reasonable extension of that line beyond the hole or any areas in which you are about to drop or place a ball, through any of the following actions:

> 66 Remember, in a hazard you can move man-made objects (movable obstructions) such as cigarette butts, empty drinks cans or candy wrappers. But you cannot move natural objects (loose impediments) such as leaves or twigs. You can't even allow the clubhead to touch them during your backswing. However, the local rules at some clubs may allow you to move stones from around your ball in a bunker, for safety reasons more than anything else. 99

• Moving, bending or breaking anything that is either growing or fixed. This includes immovable obstructions and out-of-bounds stakes. An obvious example of a breach of this rule would be violently to bend, or step on, branches in the process of taking your stance to help clear the way for an unhindered backswing. That kind of strong-arm approach is simply not acceptable. However, you can back into some branches gently if it is the *only* way of fairly taking your stance. There are subtle differences here, though, so you need to tread carefully—literally and metaphorically.

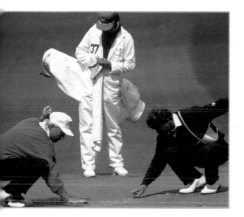

You can brush away loose sand from the putting green, but you can't do it on the fairway or even on the closely-mown fringe around the green.

• Removing or pressing down sand, loose soil, replaced divots, relayed turf, or any other irregularities of surface. You can, however, do these things on the teeing ground, or in the process of taking your stance, or indeed in the process of making a swing. So if you brush away an old divot in your backswing, for instance, that's not a problem. You can also brush away sand or loose soil on the putting green.

Repairing surface damage on the putting green is in itself a delicate subject, though, so that is covered separately.

Hazardous behavior If your ball is lying in, or touching, a hazard, you have to be very careful what you do with the club, and indeed your hands and feet. For instance, you can't test the condition of the hazard. So yes, in a bunker you are entitled to shuffle your feet into the sand to secure a firm foundation, but don't overdo it because that sort of over-zealous behavior could easily be construed as testing the surface. You can't touch the hazard with your club, either. That means no practice swings that cause the clubhead to come into contact with the hazard. Remember, this applies to everything that lies within the boundaries of the stakes indicating the hazard, so be careful when you're in, say, a grassy area bordering some water because that is then just as much a water-hazard as the water itself and therefore you cannot touch the ground with your club. There are exceptions, however. For instance if you instinctively thrust out your club, walking-stick style, to prevent yourself falling over in a hazard then, strictly speaking, that does not constitute a deliberate attempt at testing the surface of the hazard.

Rule 14 Striking the ball

To get to the heart of this matter and fully understand the rules side of "striking the ball," we need first to consider the exact definition. "A stroke is the forward momentum of the club made with the intention of fairly striking at and moving the ball, but if a player checks his downswing voluntarily before the clubhead reaches the ball, he is deemed not to have made a stroke." This explains why nudging the ball off the tee at address incurs no penalty, because there was "no intention." But let's look at some other areas of potential confusion.

Push or scoop Circumstances sometimes dictate what you can and can't do and this is one area where this rule applies. For instance, say your ball comes to rest an inch or two from a fence and you have no way of making a backswing. The definition states that the ball should be "fairly struck at" with the head of the club. But, there is no way you can make a backswing and therefore no way that you can actually strike the ball. If you were to try, you would actually be scooping, or pushing, the ball out of trouble. That is against the Rules of Golf, which will result in a one-shot penalty and the ball will have to be replaced in its original spot.

Dry state The Rules state that in playing a stroke you should not accept physical assistance or protection from the elements. This means that in pouring rain you are quite entitled to have your caddie hold an umbrella over you as you prepare to play, but once you address the ball the caddie must move away and take the umbrella with him. Equally, if you're attempting a fancy escape shot from under some overhanging branches, you can't kneel on a towel or anything like that. You just have to get your knees wet.

Double hit Striking the ball more than once is embarrassing as well as costly. Not only do you have to count both "hits," you must also add a penalty stroke. As double-hits only tend to happen when you are

66
As double hits only tend to happen when you are playing the most delicate of shots, your pain is further exaggerated by the fact that the ball has probably only traveled a few feet—and yet you have to count that as three shots.
99

playing the most delicate of shots, your pain is further exaggerated by the fact that the ball has probably only traveled a few feet—and yet you have to count that as three shots.

Moving target Playing a moving ball has rather strange consequences. If your ball falls off the tee in the middle of your backswing and you don't have the presence of mind to stop, then the chances are you are going to hit a moving ball. An air shot is the likely outcome, but if you do make contact you are not penalized under Rule 14, but you are penalized under Rule 18 and incur a one-stroke penalty. The key is to be quick-witted and stop your swing before you reach impact. Then you can simply put the ball back on its tee and start again.

Rule 15 Playing the wrong ball

Believe it or not, you don't have to strike someone else's ball to be penalized for playing the *wrong ball*. Your own ball can just as easily be the wrong ball. The rules on this point are mercifully short, and relatively sweet!

> If someone plays your ball by mistake, obviously the wrong ball for them, then provided you can catch the culprit, you simply replace the ball as close as possible to its original spot.

Basically, a wrong ball is any ball other than:

i) the ball in play

ii) a provisional ball

iii) in stroke play, a second ball played under Rule 3-3 (which relates to the situation where a golfer is unsure of a rule and thus plays out a hole with a second ball in order to obtain confirmation of a ruling after the round), or Rule 20-7b (which relates to playing a ball that has been dropped in a wrong place, but where no serious breach of the rules has occurred).

The most common acceptable excuses for *not* holing out with the ball you teed off with are: i) you replaced it under an applicable rule—it may have been damaged, for instance; or ii) you lost your original ball and have replaced it in accordance with the rules.

The penalty for playing a wrong ball is loss of hole in match play, although in a four-ball better-ball match the partner of the offending golfer is not penalized. In stroke play, it's an immediate two-stroke penalty and the golfer must then rectify the situation. That means not hitting another shot with the wrong ball and then going back to play the correct ball. This must be done before the tee shot on the next hole is struck, though, otherwise that golfer is disqualified.

> You cannot be penalized for playing a wrong ball in a hazard. Any strokes played out of a hazard with a wrong ball do not count, providing you notice your mistake and take immediate corrective action before proceeding any further.

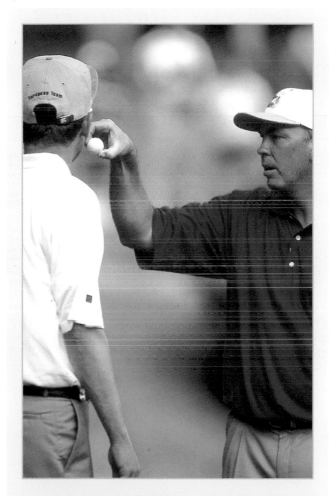

If you suspect your ball is damaged, and thus unfit for play, you must receive confirmation from your fellow competitor before you replace it with another ball.

THE PUTTING GREEN

It is on the green that you confront "the game within a game." The rules for this part of the course only go to prove that the closer you get to the hole, the more treacherous things become.

Rule 16 The putting green

There are some serious do's and don'ts when it comes to putting, and they are listed below. Ignore them at your peril.

You can:

• Lift, mark and clean your ball.

• Repair an old hole plug or pitch mark.

• Touch the line of a putt, but only in the following situations:

i) When measuring distance—for example in a closest-to-the-pin competition, or when determining whose putt it is.

ii) When placing a ball-marker in front of the ball—not likely since it's far more sensible to place the marker behind the ball.

iii) When repairing pitch marks or old hole plugs.

iv) When removing a movable obstruction or loose impediment, with either your hand or the clubhead.

You cannot:

- Touch the line of a putt except in the situations just outlined.

- Test the surface of the green by rolling a ball or scraping the surface.

- Stand astride, or on, the line of a putt.

- Play your ball while another ball is in motion.

- Touch the green when indicating the line of your partner's putt.

- Brush aside early morning dew or frost from the line of your putt.

- Wait for an age for your ball to drop if it hangs agonizingly over the edge of the hole. All you've got is the time it takes you to get to the hole and 10 seconds once you are there—no longer than that, and no jumping up and down by the hole-side!

There was a time when the "stymie" rule required you to find a way round a ball interfering with play on the putting green, but today you can simply have the ball marked and lifted.

Rule 17 The flagstick

This is what every golfer aims for, but there's more to the flagstick than meets the eye. It can get you into real trouble.

When you're off the green you have three choices as to what to do with the flagstick. You can have it left in, you can have it taken out, or you can have it attended. If you go for the latter of the three options and your ball then hits the flagstick, you suffer a two-stroke penalty, so make sure your "attender" is paying attention.

> "All you've got is the time it takes you to get to the hole and 10 seconds once you are there—no longer than that, and no jumping up and down by the hole-side."

If you are on the green, your options are reduced to two. You can have the flag attended (with the same implications as outlined above) or you can have the flag out. Bear in mind, though, that just because the flag is out doesn't mean to say it's not a danger to your score. It is, and if your ball hits it while it's lying on the ground, you've got a two-stroke penalty on your hands.

There is one final interesting point about having the flag attended. If you are playing to an elevated green and can't see part, or indeed all, of the flagstick, you are entitled to ask someone to hold the flagstick high in the air directly above the hole to guide you to your target. That person can even stay put, holding the flag aloft, as you play your shot—a rare case of generosity from the Rules of Golf.

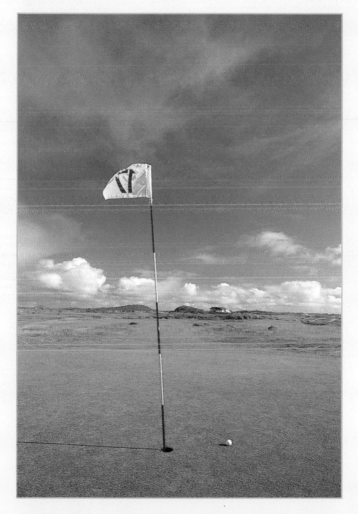

A sight to lift the spirits of any golfer, but make sure you know what to do with the flagstick once you get to the green.

BALL AT REST, MOVED OR DEFLECTED

Once a ball stops moving, you'd think its resting place would be assured. Not quite. Anything can happen after the ball has stopped...and sometimes does. It pays to know what to do when the unlikely becomes reality.

Rule 18 Ball at rest moved

The definition states that a ball at rest is officially deemed to have moved when it leaves its position and comes to rest in another spot. Which, remember, is why a ball merely oscillating in the wind does not constitute a ball moved. Really, the crux of this rule is what caused the ball to move.

Stop thief! If an outside agency causes your ball to move after it has come to rest, then you may simply drop it as close to its original resting place as you can accurately determine. If your ball was originally on the green, you may place it on its spot. Examples of an outside agency would be a cat, a crow, or a squirrel, it might even be the greenskeeper out mowing the fairways. If the outside agency is a cunning or successful thief—amazingly, it is quite common for a crow to fly off with a ball in its beak—then, frustrating though it may be, you can simply replace it with another and proceed as normal.

Be careful The rules are less forgiving in other instances involving your ball at rest being moved. Basically, if it is moved by you, your caddie, or a piece of equipment belonging to you or your partner, you immediately incur a penalty of one stroke. You must then replace the ball on its original spot and play on from there.

In the clear You are not penalized, however, if you accidentally move your ball in any of the following circumstances:

• Measuring to determine which ball is furthest from the hole—a common requirement on the putting green.

- Searching for a covered ball in a hazard, casual water or ground under repair.

- In the process of repairing a hole plug or pitch mark on the green.

- While removing a loose impediment on the putting green.

- While lifting, placing or replacing a ball as necessary in the course of taking relief from an applicable rule.

- During the course of lifting a ball that is either interfering with, or assisting, play.

- While clearing a movable obstruction out of the way.

Ball moving after address If your ball moves after you've addressed it (other than as the result of a stroke, of course) you are held responsible and thus incur a one-stroke penalty. The ball then needs to be replaced on its original spot. The exception to this is when a ball moves mid-swing and, not having the presence of mind to stop yourself, you despatch it several hundred yards down the fairway. That doesn't get you off the hook, though. You have to add a penalty stroke for hitting a moving ball, and then proceed from where the ball has come to rest.

Danger on the loose If you are attempting to move any loose impediments lying within a club-length of your ball and that action causes your ball to move, you are penalized one stroke. The only time you can get away with this is on the putting green, when the same action moves your ball or your ball-marker. Each time, though, you have to replace the ball on its original spot before you proceed.

On the lookout Searching for your ball in the rough is another potentially hazardous business. It doesn't matter if your opponent or your fellow competitor stumbles on the ball by accident—you simply thank them for finding it and put it back in its original resting place. If it's you who kicks the ball, though, you are penalized. It's a tough break, so it pays to tread carefully when you are looking for your ball.

BALL IN MOTION, DEFLECTED OR STOPPED

If a ball at rest can be knocked off its spot when you least expect it, then so can a ball that has yet to complete its journey. And we're not talking about garden-variety bad bounces and deflections off trees. It can get much, much more intriguing than that.

Rule 19 Ball in motion, deflected or stopped

First the good news.

Rub of the green If your ball in motion is deflected or stopped by an outside agency, then that is known as a rub of the green and you play the ball as it lies. So if your ball hits the greenskeeper's tractor and bounces on to the green two feet from the pin, then you are in luck. But the bad news is that the rub of the green can also work against you. If your ball deflects off that same piece of equipment and over the out-of-bounds fence, there's nothing you can do about it. It's tough. You have to treat it just as you would any other "OB-situation."

Animal interference If you hit a shot and the ball, while still in motion, gets carried away—say by a dog, or a squirrel picks it up and runs off with it (don't laugh, it has been known to happen)—then you replace that ball as close to the spot where the animal first grabbed it and play on from there without penalty. If you're on the green, though, and your putt is interfered with on its journey to the hole, then you should cancel the stroke and play it again from the original spot. Once again, if the thief makes a clean getaway with your ball you can simply substitute it with another.

Don't touch If your ball is deflected or stopped while in motion, either by you, your partner or your equipment, or indeed either of your caddies, then you lose that hole in match play. In stroke play you incur a two-stroke penalty and then have to play the ball as it lies. If, however, your ball hits your opponent, or your fellow competitor, or their equipment or caddies, there is no penalty incurred by anyone—providing it is an accident, of course. What then happens is that you choose either to play it as it lies, or cancel the stroke altogether and play the stroke again. If you take the latter option, you must replay the stroke before another shot is played by either party.

Balls collide If you hit a shot and your ball collides with another ball at rest, there is no penalty—although it might hurt a bit if your ball was heading straight for the hole—you simply play the ball as it lies.

> Be careful where you leave your golf bag around the green. If you hit a shot out of a greenside bunker and it flies past the pin and hits your golf bag, you are penalized two strokes. Either that or you lose the hole in match play. So make sure you don't leave it on an extension of the line of play; it may cost you dearly.

■ *This lady is officially an "outside agency" and therefore Curtis Strange will mark the position of his ball, ask her to move, then replace the ball as close as possible to its original resting place.*

The important exception to this, however, is when both balls are on the putting green, in which case the player who struck the ball is the guilty party. So if you hit a putt and it collides with a ball at rest, also on the putting green, you are penalized. That's why it pays to ask for a fellow competitor's or opponent's ball to be marked, even if there's only the remotest chance that you might hit it. Let's face it, hitting a wild putt is bad enough without also having to swallow a two-stroke penalty, or loss of hole in match play, for your ball striking another on the putting green

RELIEF SITUATIONS AND PROCEDURES

If you make a mistake, or find yourself in a sticky situation, you can compound the problem by not knowing the correct procedures. Conversely, a thorough knowledge of these laws can help ease you out of a tight spot. It's better to be smart than sorry.

Rule 20 Lifting and dropping

Any time you're thinking about lifting, dropping, placing or replacing a ball you're in a very vulnerable position. A moment's impetuosity is all it takes to land you in trouble.

Lifting with care The only time you can lift a ball without fear of rules retribution is when you pluck it out of the hole. At any other time you must mark the position of the ball before you even touch it. If you don't do that, you will incur an immediate one-stroke penalty—not a good start to your relief procedure. If for some reason you move the marker in the process of lifting the ball, then there is no penalty providing you instantly replace the marker on its spot.

Dropping a clanger The procedure for dropping a ball—whether it's a free drop or a penalty drop—is simple. You stand upright, with your arm extended at shoulder height, and let the ball drop. You can drop it to the side of you or in front of you, but you mustn't throw it—just let gravity take its course. Again, just by adopting an incorrect style you incur a penalty of one stroke, so make sure you do it right. If the ball hits you, either on the way

> 66 You can use virtually anything to mark your ball on the green, although a small coin is the sensible option. If that marker then interferes with another player's line of putt, it is polite to offer to move it. This can be done by measuring to one side with the aid of your putter-head. Just remember to put your marker back on its original spot before you replace the ball. 99

down or after it has bounced, you may re-drop without penalty. The same rule applies if the ball strikes your caddie, your golf bag, or even your partner. There's no limit to the number of times you can re-drop under those circumstances.

Drop zone A ball should never be dropped nearer the hole. That rule is set in stone. But what situations dictate whether or not you should *re-drop*? Well, amazingly there are seven possible scenarios where a drop has to be followed by a re-drop. These are:

1 If the ball rolls into a hazard.

2 If the ball rolls out of a hazard—you obviously have to be in a hazard in the first place.

■ *You must drop a ball in the correct fashion, standing upright with your arm extended at shoulder height.*

3 If the ball rolls onto the putting green. If you were on the putting green in the first place you wouldn't be required to drop the ball, merely place it.

4 If the ball rolls out of bounds—it would be harsh if you weren't allowed to re-drop under circumstances as unfortunate as that.

5 If the ball rolls back into a position where it is affected by either an immovable obstruction or some abnormal ground condition from which you were taking relief in the first place. Again, that makes perfect sense.

6 If the ball comes to rest more than two club-lengths from the spot where it first struck the ground.

7 If the ball comes to rest nearer the hole.

However, in all seven situations, re-dropping is not a never-ending process. Once you have re-dropped once—that's two drops in total—you must then place it as near as possible to the spot where it first struck the ground. If, for some reason, the ball rolls off into a non-recoverable position, it may have disappeared down an animal burrow perhaps, then you can substitute that ball with another without penalty.

Rule 20 Placing, replacing and playing from the wrong place

Okay, we're still on Rule 20—it's a lengthy section, with dozens of very relevant and realistic scenarios.

Placing and replacing It's best if you are the one who replaces your own ball. Your partner can do it for you, say in a four-ball match, but you are the one who takes the rap when something goes wrong—take control of the situation yourself and save any partnership-wrecking incidents. It's worth reiterating a point made earlier. If a ball-marker is moved, or indeed if the ball itself is moved, in the process of marking that ball or replacing it, then you are not penalized. But you must put the marker back on its original spot before you play your next stroke. Obviously it might be difficult to determine the exact spot, down to the nearest hair's-breadth, but you must attempt to place it as near as possible to what you feel was the original spot. It's a one-stroke penalty if you get it wrong.

Original lies The rules are fair and, rightly, you are entitled to the lie you are given, good or bad. If the lie of a ball that you are about to replace, is altered in some way then that is not right. So providing you are not in a hazard you can place the ball in the nearest lie most similar to the original lie, up to one club-length away and no nearer the hole.

If you are in a bunker, then you have to try to recreate the original lie as best you can and replace the ball on that spot. This kind of situation can easily arise if, say, two balls come to rest very close together in the sand

■ *Having marked and lifted his bunkered ball to allow a fellow competitor to play a shot, Tiger Woods checks to see that it is restored to the original lie.*

and one of you has to mark your ball in order for the other golfer to play the shot without interference. That's obviously going to destroy your original lie—either with footprints or by the clubhead splashing through the sand—so it is only fair that you should be entitled to recreate the original lie. Don't use this as an opportunity to give yourself a better lie, though. If the ball was half-buried in the first place, then half-buried it must be before you play your shot.

Moving ball If a ball won't stay on its spot every time you try to replace it, then you have to use your initiative and find a spot no nearer the hole where the ball will stay put. Strangely, this is not an uncommon scenario, especially on fast-sloping greens or, say, severely contoured fairways. You should involve your opponent or fellow competitor when replacing a ball, just to ensure there is agreement about what is a fair place on which to replace the ball.

Wrong time, wrong place Playing a shot from the wrong place incurs a two-shot penalty, or a loss of hole in match play. Worse still, if you then don't take immediate corrective action in accordance with the rules you are disqualified. The real danger situation is when you have to play a shot from the spot where your previous shot was played (an example would

be if you have knocked a ball out of bounds) or if you have elected to cancel a previous stroke and play it again (say you hit a putt that was deflected by your opponent's putter, which had inadvertently been left on the ground). The procedures vary depending on where you are on the course. If you are on the tee, then anywhere within the two tee-markers is acceptable—you don't have to go to the exact spot from where you hit the previous shot. If you are on the putting green, you place the ball as close as possible to its original spot, rather than drop it. And if you are anywhere else on the course, or in a hazard, you drop it, again as close as possible to the spot from which you played the previous stroke. This can be harsh if you are dropping in a bunker, because the ball will obviously plug to some extent, but that's a tough break you will just have to accept.

Rule 21 Cleaning your ball

Don't take anything for granted on this rule. Your ball may have the most ridiculous lump of mud stuck to it, but don't assume you can just go ahead and clean it off, because in some situations it isn't that simple. Here's what you can and can't do:

You can clean your ball once it has come to rest on the putting green. Indeed, it is advisable to do so because even the smallest piece of grit or dirt trapped at impact between clubface and ball can completely ruin a putt. Let's face it, putting is hard enough, without this complicating matters.

Elsewhere on the course:

You can't clean your ball when you have lifted it in the process of determining whether it is damaged or, in other words, unfit for play.

You can clean your ball in the process of identifying it, if it is strictly necessary. But once you've cleaned off enough mud, or whatever else is stuck to the ball, to be able to confirm that it is yours, you then have to stop right there. You can't go on cleaning it until it is whiter than the driven snow!

You can't clean your ball if you have just lifted it because it interferes with play. This might occur when two balls come to rest side by side on the fairway, for instance. Sure you can mark and lift one of the balls to allow one of you to play a shot, but the ball has to go back on the ground in the exact state it was in before—muddy or not.

You can't clean your ball if it's sitting pretty in the middle of the fairway, but has a lump of mud stuck to it. Yes, it might alter the flight characteristics of the ball, but that's something you have to live with until your ball has safely come to rest on the putting green. Then you can mark, lift and clean it.

66

Here's a strange anomaly, the kind that the rules of golf occasionally bring up. A dead insect stuck to your ball, or more likely the remnants of one, cannot be removed "through the green." But a live insect can be cleaned off, because it is not considered to be adhering to the ball. You have to be careful, though, either delicately removing it or blowing it off. You can't lift the ball unless provided for in one of the cases listed above.

99

Rule 22 Ball interfering with, or assisting, play

In the old days, and we're going back something like half-a-century here, there was a rule called the "stymie." Basically this meant that if a ball was in your way on the putting green, it was your problem. You had to find a way to the hole by either going around or over it—hardly what could be described as fair. Not surprisingly, the rule was eventually dropped.

■ When two balls come to rest so close to one another on the green, it can be tricky figuring out the easiest course of action to avoid interference.

Today, thankfully, there are rules designed to provide a more equitable solution to situations in which one ball is influencing in some way the play of another ball. Obviously the position of a ball can have either a positive or a negative effect on you, depending on the circumstance, and therefore there are two sides to this coin.

Assistance Nobody likes to give away an advantage, so you are perfectly entitled to lift and mark your ball if you feel it will provide some form of assistance to any

other player in your group. Indeed, in a stroke play event you are entitled to play first rather than lift and mark, if you so wish. You do not have this option in match play.

Interference Equally, you do not deserve to be hampered by the location of another golfer's ball. So you are entitled to ask for another ball to be marked and lifted if you feel it interferes with your play. This doesn't only apply to physical interference, either. It can be the mental kind, too. For instance, if you are preparing to putt and find that a ball lying to the side, but nowhere near the line of play, is catching your eye and distracting you then you can ask for it to be marked.

Bear in mind, however, that unless the ball is on the putting green, it cannot be cleaned when lifted. The penalty for any breach of rule 22 is the familiar loss of hole in match play, or a two-stroke penalty in a stroke play competition.

> " In theory, two devious golfers in a stroke play event could come to some mutual agreement to leave in place any ball that assists the other in some way. For example, a ball lying six inches beyond the hole would be a useful "back-stop" for a golfer faced with a nasty, downhill chip. Don't even think about pulling this kind of stunt, though. If there's proof of this sort of behavior, it will mean immediate disqualification. "

Rule 23 Loose impediments

Mention the words "loose impediment" to the average golfer and you'll probably be met with a pretty vacant expression. It's not surprising, really, because superficially it is a fairly nondescript term. That's why it's best to refer to loose impediments by their more common term, *natural objects*. Natural objects means what it says—leaves, twigs, branches, stones, pine cones, apple cores, banana skins, that sort of thing. You might not have known where to look for a loose impediment, but natural objects...well, they're all over the golf course.

> A dislodged divot is a loose impediment, so you can move it from around your ball if you want to. But if that same divot is resting in its original home, the divot hole, it is not a loose impediment and therefore can't be moved

Indeed they are, which is why it is imperative that you know how to deal with natural objects whenever you and your golf ball come in contact with them. The good news is that, providing the natural object isn't fixed or growing and isn't solidly embedded in the ground or stuck to the ball, nor is the object or the ball in a hazard, you can move it without penalty. Be very careful, though. If the ball moves while you're merrily going about the business of moving the loose impediment, you will suffer a one-stroke penalty. You've also got to make sure you replace the ball on its spot before you play your next shot.

It is essential, therefore, that before you even consider moving a natural object from around your golf ball, you ensure the ball will not move in the process. If there's even the slightest doubt, don't touch a thing because it's not worth the risk.

All clear? Good, because wouldn't you know it, there are some other, less clear-cut, issues to consider concerning loose impediments, or natural objects. For example, sand and loose soil *are* classified as loose impediments on the green and therefore may be brushed away. But off the green, sand and soil suddenly *are not* classified as loose impediments and therefore cannot be moved.

■ *A fall day will call upon even the likes of Jack Nicklaus to do some gardening, since the rules permit leaves to be brushed away from the line of a putt.*

As for snow…well, if you are intrepid enough to be out on the course in that kind of weather, you have a choice. You can call snow a loose impediment, in which case you can brush it away from around your ball; or you can call it casual water, in which case you can take a free drop to the nearest point of relief—which is likely to be the clubhouse! The same rules and procedures apply to ice. Strangely, though, the rules aren't so generous in the case of frost—you just have to live with that ground condition and play the ball as it lies.

Well and truly bunkered Remember, loose impediments are movable. But not when you are in a hazard. So if by some misfortune your ball plummets into a bunker and comes to rest against a fallen branch the size of your arm, sadly that is just a bad "rub of the green." You can't move the branch—you have to play ball as it lies. With stones, however, it's sometimes a different story. At many golf clubs a local rule exists whereby in a bunker you can remove stones from around your ball. Clearly that's a nod toward safety, because a sharp-edged steel clubhead crashing into a stone at 60mph could have very nasty consequences. That's a sensible Local Rule, but again you have to be very careful that you don't physically improve the lie of your ball when removing a stone from the sand.

Rule 24 Obstructions

Here is another instance of a term that isn't immediately obvious. As with the previous rule, things start to make a lot more sense if you call it by another name—artificial objects, perhaps. In no time at all you can think of all sorts of artificial objects that can be found on a golf course. Empty drinks cans, cigarette butts, a bunker rake, a pop-up sprinkler head—all these objects fall under the all-encompassing term "obstructions." But within this category there are, in fact, two types of obstruction. Should you come across them on the golf course, the treatment of each is completely different. So let's deal with each separately.

A golf buggy is an example of a movable obstruction. If the ball moves while the buggy is being driven away, it must be placed as close as possible to its original spot.

Movable obstruction

Obviously this applies to obstructions that you can move, such as the drinks can or bunker rake. If your ball comes to rest against one of these, or near enough for it to cause an obstruction, you are entitled to move it out of the way in order to play your shot without hindrance. If the ball itself moves while you're in the process of shifting the obstruction, there's no need to panic as there is no penalty. You simply place the ball back on its original spot.

> 66 Stakes, posts or a fence indicating out-of-bounds are artificial objects, but you are not entitled to the relief offered with other obstructions. So if your ball is just in bounds, but your stance or swing is impeded by the indicators marking the out of bounds, then you have to play it as it lies or take a penalty drop. 99

You can make life easier for yourself, though, if you try to anticipate when your ball might move in these circumstances. This will allow you the luxury of marking with a tee-peg the exact position of the ball before you start to move the obstruction. Should the ball move off its spot, then you are spared any embarrassing confusion or debate about its original position. It's the smallest of details, but this kind of forethought can make all the difference in delicate situations.

If the ball is lying on a movable obstruction, or perhaps even in it, which is obviously quite possible, then you are required to lift the ball before you move the obstruction. Again, though, you should mark the original position of the ball. In doing so you are removing as much doubt as possible. Once the area is cleared, you must drop the ball as near as possible to the spot where the ball would have been resting had the obstruction not been there in the first place. If you are on the green, you can place it on its spot.

In both instances you are allowed to clean your ball when it is lifted. The rules concerning movable obstructions are equally applicable when your ball lies in a hazard, such as a bunker for instance. Here you are allowed to move out of the way any movable obstructions. Remember, though, if the ball moves in the process you have to return it in the appropriate manner to its original spot. Any breach of the rules relating to movable obstructions carries a penalty of two strokes, or the loss of hole in match play.

Rule 24 Obstructions

Now let's look at the second category of artificial object and the necessary relief procedures when you or your ball encounter one.

> If there is good evidence to suggest that your ball is lost in an immovable obstruction, you are allowed to substitute another ball and take relief in the appropriate way—in other words, drop the ball within one club-length of the nearest point of relief, no nearer the hole. However, this ruling doesn't apply to immovable obstructions that lie in water hazards.

Immovable obstructions

This relates to artificial objects that you can't physically move—such as a fixed pop-up sprinkler head by the side of a green, or the "tombstone-style" structures on the side of each teeing area giving information about the hole. The good news is that you are entitled to relief from immovable obstructions. And since we've established that you can't move the obstruction, this means that you have to move your ball instead.

Before you can take relief, though, you must first prove that there is actual interference from the immovable obstruction. Being in the way of your ball's intended flight path is not a good enough reason. The obstruction must physically interfere in the sense that it either stops you from taking up your normal stance or from making an unimpeded swing, or the ball is touching the obstruction or so close to it that it represents an actual problem.

Only then can you go ahead and move your ball into the clear, so to speak, and you have to be very precise about where you move it. If your ball lies "through the green" (anywhere on the course other than in a hazard or on the putting green, not *through the green,* as in beyond the putting surface) then you must find the nearest spot, no nearer the hole, where the immovable obstruction ceases to be an obstruction. Mark the position with a tee-peg and drop your ball within one club-length of that spot. It's worth stressing again that you cannot drop the ball nearer the hole and you can't drop it on the putting green or, you'll be relieved to learn, into a hazard.

However, if you are in a bunker in the first place and are claiming relief from an immovable obstruction (a highly unlikely scenario), you do have to drop the ball in the hazard.

One particular point worth mentioning is the potential gray area that could arise when determining whether or not an immovable obstruction is actually a legitimate obstruction. By that I mean you can't adopt the most ridiculous stance, with your feet miles apart, and them claim physical interference in order to get yourself out of a tight spot that you don't fancy playing from. To get relief in this way you have to be taking your normal stance. Likewise your normal swing must be impeded for there to be a legitimate reason for taking relief—it's no use rehearsing bizarre, wild, looping movements and then claiming an obstruction. That's not legal— and it's definitely not in the spirit of the game, either.

■ *A Local Rule at Lahinch Golf Club in Ireland would deem this marker stone an immovable obstruction, offering relief should it interfere with stance or swing. The same would apply to this distance marker on of one of Valderrama's fairways.*

ABNORMAL GROUND CONDITIONS

This is an all-encompassing heading since "abnormal ground conditions" could apply to virtually anything. Golf courses being the fairly manicured areas of land that they are, though, it is actually quite a concise definition which applies to only a handful of "earthy" scenarios.

Rule 25 Casual water

This is probably the single most common abnormal ground condition, although if you play most of your golf in a region that enjoys more than its fair share of rain you might think it isn't that abnormal. The official definition, however, is a "temporary accumulation of water on the golf course which is visible before or after the player takes his stance." A puddle on the golf course is easy to spot and an obvious case of casual water. But even if you can't see the casual water when you get to your ball, it doesn't necessarily mean you can't claim relief. Sometimes it is the player just standing to the ball that brings the water to the surface—and that's good enough. You can claim relief for that.

You can't jump up and down around the ball in order to try to force some water to the surface. You must merely address your ball as normal.

You can claim casual water for snow or ice, though, since these two natural conditions are classed as both casual water *and* loose impediments. Which option you choose to take in a relief situation is entirely up to you.

Taking relief So what are the procedures, then, when you have established that it is casual water? Well first you must look for the nearest point of relief—in other words, an area of completely dry land—that is no nearer the hole. Mark that spot with a tee-peg, measure out one club length from there and mark that spot with another tee-peg. You then simply drop the ball within the two tee-pegs. Don't forget that you are not required to re-drop if the ball rolls up to another two club-lengths away, providing the ball first bounced within your designated one-club-length area and does not come to rest nearer the hole.

On the green Previously we've said that casual water must affect either your stance or the lie of your ball. Well, on the putting surface it's a different story. Obviously you can still claim relief if the water is around your ball or your stance. However, you can also claim relief if the line of your putt is affected by standing water. You'll be glad to know that the Rules of Golf don't expect you to have to putt through puddles! In these instances you must identify a spot on the green where the line to the hole is not troubled by water. Once you've figured that out, mark the original position of your ball and place it on the spot where you've established there is a dry line to the hole. Before proceeding, check with a player in your group that the original spot and the new spot are equidistant from the hole.

You can't take a ball from casual water and drop it on the green if the ball wasn't on the green in the first place.

Water in a bunker As any rules expert will tell you, a waterlogged bunker is one of the least "fair" situations you'll ever encounter. It's not so bad if some of the sand is still showing, although dropping a ball in a bunker inevitably results in a semi-buried lie. The trouble starts when your ball finishes in a completely waterlogged bunker. Then you have two options, neither of which is the least bit appealing.

i) You can drop it in the shallowest area of water within the bunker, which means you not only face an incredibly tough shot, but also the prospect of getting wet. The one upside is that this is a free-drop.

ii) You drop outside the bunker, no nearer the hole, on an extension of the imaginary line between flag and the spot where the ball originally came to rest in the sand. This second option incurs a one-stroke penalty and, as if to add insult to injury, inevitably means you have to chip over the bunker.

Rule 25 Ground under repair and other abnormal ground conditions

Again we're still on the same rule, but this part deals with ground under repair, a condition that you'll find somewhere on every golf course at some time or other, plus several other situations where the lie of your ball, or your stance is...well, abnormal.

Ground under repair This is easy to spot on the golf course because it is usually marked as such by a white-painted line and the enormous letters "GUR." Some areas that qualify as ground under repair might not be marked, though. For instance, a hole dug by the greenskeeper, or some sliced turf that has been piled for collection. These should be treated in the same way. Taking relief from ground under repair is identical in procedure to that of casual water. You must identify the nearest point where the condition ceases to become an interference and then drop the ball within one club-length of that spot. It's probably obvious by now, but worth mentioning again, that you *cannot drop the ball any nearer the hole.*

Plugged ball This is a common occurrence in winter and yet thousands of golfers do not know the proper procedure when a golf ball "plugs" in its own pitch mark. On *any closely mown* area of grass it's simple. There's no penalty involved. You can mark and lift the ball, clean it if necessary and drop it as close as possible to its original spot—no questions asked.

The possible uncertain area occurs when your ball plugs in its own pitch mark *in the rough.* In that situation the Rules of Golf do not actually allow you to lift, clean and drop without penalty. In the winter months many committees will extend the "relief area" to include rough, but you have to make very sure you know your facts before you unplug your ball. These decisions are known as Local Rules and later in the book we cover them in more detail.

Wrong green If your ball ends up on the green of a hole you are not playing, then it makes sense that you can't play from there. What you must do is drop the ball to the nearest side of the green, which is actually a nice break because you'll probably get a perfect lie on the closely-mown "apron." One more thing: a practice putting green is also classified as a wrong green so you have to drop away from that, too.

Animals It's only fair that you shouldn't have to pay the price for the nocturnal mischief of the local wildlife. So if your ball, your stance, or even your swing is affected by a burrow or a hole that has obviously been made by an animal, you are allowed to take relief from that area. Again, find the nearest point of relief and drop the ball within one club-length of that spot. If your ball was in a hazard to start with, you must drop the ball within that hazard.

Disappearing ball This one can pose a tough decision, but you just have to be sensible. The critical point is that there must be reasonable evidence to suggest that a ball is indeed lost in an abnormal ground condition—such as casual water or ground under repair. Once you have that consensus of opinion, the relief procedure is really quite straightforward. First, substitute the missing ball. Then without penalty, drop it no nearer the hole and within one club-length of a spot that is outside the affected area, on an extension of the line formed by the flag and the actual point where the ball crossed the margin of the affected area.

Any time you breach a rule concerning ground under repair, casual water, or any of the other abnormal ground conditions mentioned in this section, you face a two-stroke penalty, or the loss of that hole in match play.

WATER HAZARDS

Water is water as far as your golf ball is concerned—one splash is much the same as any other! But the rules don't see it that way. There are actually two types of water on the golf course—a water hazard and a lateral water hazard, and each determines what course of action you take when your ball goes for a swim.

Rule 26 Water hazards

The easiest way to determine if your ball has just dived into a water hazard is by looking at the colored stakes or painted lines indicating the margins of the hazard itself. These should be yellow. The important point to note from the outset is that everything within this border is part of the hazard, which means you can often find yourself on dry land and yet officially *in* a water hazard.

Before you can do anything, you have to establish beyond reasonable doubt that your ball went in the hazard. Obviously if you find your ball lying in shallow water, or in the grass bordering the hazard and within the yellow lines, no further proof is necessary. But if your ball is not found, you have to come to a conclusion

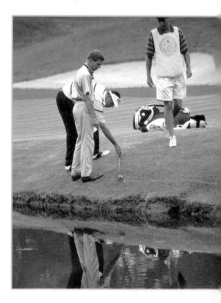

■ *There are many courses of action open to you should your ball find a water hazard. Consider them carefully before you make your move.*

> Remember, you cannot ground your club in any grassy area surrounding a water hazard that falls within the boundaries of the yellow lines or stakes. Neither can you make a practice swing in which the club comes into contact with the grass or the ground.

with your fellow competitors or your opponent that there is reasonable evidence to support the fact that the ball finished in the water hazard. Once that has been decided are you entitled to choose one of the three relief options open to you.

Relief option No.1 If you can find it, you are allowed to play it. That's not so tough if the ball is lying in the grass surrounding the hazard, although you can't ground your club. But it's a whole different game if your ball is submerged. Even if you can see the ball clearly you have to think very carefully about taking this on, because even water that is perhaps as little as three or four inches deep can make an escape shot very hazardous. You'll certainly get soaked. Worse still, you could easily leave the ball in the water and then you're really up to your neck in trouble—albeit probably only metaphorically speaking!

Relief option No.2 Drop a ball behind the water hazard. Not just anywhere, though. You are required to be precise about where you take the penalty drop. What you must do is identify a line between the flag and the spot where your ball first crossed the margin of the water hazard—a point of entry, so to speak. Then you extend that line back away from the flag and drop the ball on that line. There is no limit to how far back you can go and you get a one-shot penalty for your troubles.

Relief option No.3 Go back to the spot from where you played your last shot, a penalty often referred to simply as "stroke-and-distance." This is probably the last resort, since the punishment is perhaps the most severe of the three. If you've hit your second shot on a par-4 into water, you then go back to the spot where you hit that shot and play your fourth from there. Hence the label stroke-and-distance—add a stroke to your score and forfeit the distance the ball traveled.

Rule 26   Lateral water hazards

Lateral water hazards are indicated by red stakes or painted lines. This type of water was given a separate definition by the rule-makers, and very wisely so, to cover situations where it simply isn't possible to proceed under Relief Option No.2 outlined on the previous page. You can still plump for any one of the first three options, but the rules also permit you to choose from one of two further options.

You can drop a ball outside the lateral water hazard, within two club-lengths of the point where your ball crossed the margin of the hazard—the point of entry. That's a one-stroke penalty. Or you can identify a spot on the opposite side of the water hazard, again no nearer the hole, and drop the ball within two club-lengths of that point. Again, a one-stroke penalty.

What is enough evidence   You have to be strict with yourself on this matter. Two examples help illustrate the point. Let's say a water hazard is surrounded by nothing but closely-mown fairway and light rough. If you can't find your ball, then there is reasonable evidence to suggest that the ball is indeed lost in the water hazard. If, however, the water hazard nestles among bushes, trees or tall grass, that's a different story. You really could not say for certain where your ball might have finished. If you saw a splash, well that's probably good enough, but don't forget that a low-flying golf ball can skim across water. It's all down to common sense and, above all, integrity. If you really aren't certain that the ball finished in the water hazard, then you have to treat it as an ordinary lost ball.

> In case you haven't noticed by now, a penalty drop gives you two club-lengths to work in and a free drop gives you one club-length.

The penalty for not abiding by the rules is two strokes when you're playing in a stroke play event and loss of hole in match play—hardly the sort of encouragement you will want to give to your grateful opponent.

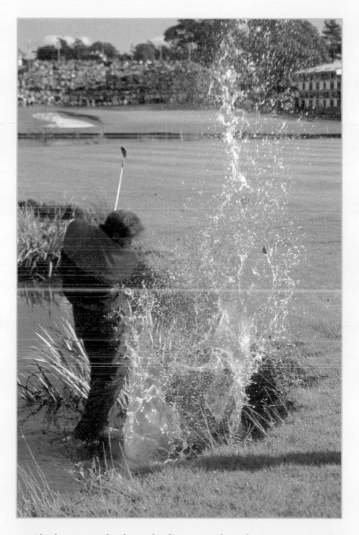

■ *It's a brave man who plays a shot from a water hazard—even Payne Stewart failed to get the ball back on dry land at the first, or even the second, attempt.*

Rule 27 Lost ball; out-of-bounds; and provisional ball

It doesn't take long after setting foot on a golf course to realize that there are more than enough opportunities to lose a ball. Too many, it seems, when you're a novice. So after cursing your swing, your ball, your bad luck, or perhaps all three, what exactly do you do about a lost ball?

When is a ball a lost ball? Well, that's not as simple a question as you might think. By definition, your ball is deemed lost if: a) It is not found and identified within five minutes of starting to look for it; b) You have put another ball in play in accordance with an applicable rule; and c) You have played a stroke with a provisional ball from a point which is either level with, or beyond, your original ball.

Out of bounds This is usually indicated by white stakes or a white line, but not always. If it's a boundary of the golf course it may simply be a fence, but it will still be indicated as out of bounds on the back of the score card. Whatever, out of bounds is a total no-go area. Of course, there is nothing to stop you from retrieving the ball, but you can't play a stroke from an area designated as out of bounds. You have to take a stroke-and-distance penalty, which means adding a stroke to your score and then going back as close as possible to the spot from where you played the offending stroke.

Provisional ball This is what you hit when you suspect that you may have lost a ball with your previous stroke. By playing a provisional you're basically saying "that first ball might be lost, so if we can't find it then this second ball will become the ball in play." If you then don't find your original ball within the allotted five-minutes search time, you add a penalty stroke and continue to play on from the spot where your provisional ball came to rest. You can continue to play a provisional ball up to the point where you think the original ball might be, but if you play a shot with a provisional ball from beyond that point, in other words nearer the hole, that ball is the ball in play and your original ball is officially lost. Even if you subsequently find the original, you can't play it. You forfeit that right by playing a shot with your provisional ball from a point nearer the hole.

You are *not allowed* to play a provisional ball if your ball may be lost in a water hazard. But any other time you think your ball is a "gonner" it is positively recommended that you play a provisional, as much for the time-saving benefits as anything else. Make sure you say as much before you actually play a provisional ball, otherwise that ball immediately becomes the ball in play—and even if you find your original ball you won't be allowed to play it.

> 66 A lost ball isn't always the end of the world. Given enough reasonable evidence, you are not penalized if your ball is lost in certain abnormal ground conditions, such as casual water or ground under repair. Nor are you subject to penalty if your ball is lost in an immovable obstruction, providing that obstruction does not lie in a water hazard. In all of these cases you can substitute the lost ball and follow the appropriate relief procedures without suffering a penalty. 99

■ *Sometimes you don't need to be told where you can't go to play your next shot (left). At other times, out of bounds is determined by a matter of fractions (above).*

Rule 28 Ball unplayable

Since there are vast differences in playing ability between golfers, the term "ball unplayable" is a completely gray area. A ball that one golfer may consider to be totally unplayable could simply be a slight inconvenience for the low-handicap golfer. Since the rule book doesn't know how good a player you are, it rightly advocates that only you can truly decide whether or not your ball is unplayable. "Ball unplayable" is one rule which is totally your call.

> If you're dropping from an unplayable lie and your ball rolls back into another unplayable lie, it's tough. You can't re-drop without penalty. You just have to treat is as another unplayable lie. And that is painful, so think before you drop!

Putting aside any debates, let's assume your ball has come to rest in a thick gorse bush so prickly that you can barely get to it let alone play it. You don't like the look of it, so you say to your fellow competitor that you are declaring the ball unplayable. What happens next?

Well, you've got three choices. First, you can return to the spot from where you played your last shot— a stroke-and-distance penalty. Second, you can drop a ball within two club-lengths of the spot where the ball was declared unplayable—measure out this distance with your driver and mark the spot with a tee-peg. And third, you can identify an imaginary line between the flag and your ball, then drop the ball on an extension of that line, obviously further away from the hole. Each of these three options involves a one-stroke penalty.

Unplayable in sand The rules change slightly if you're in a bunker and decide to declare your ball unplayable. The stroke-and-distance option is still open to you, but the second and third options have to be exercised within the confines of the bunker. Which means that you can drop the ball within two club-lengths of the unplayable lie, but only as long as you drop the ball in the sand. And yes, you can drop on an extension of the ball-to-flag line, but again only as far back as keeps you in the sand. Since dropping a ball in sand usually results in a semi-buried lie for your next shot, you need to be doubly-alert when considering your options in a bunker.

Committees have an obligation to advise of dangerous situations (left). Seve Ballesteros unsuccessfully tries to obtain relief during the 1994 Volvo Masters at Valderrama (above).

Water doesn't count

A water hazard is the only place on the golf course where you can't declare your ball unplayable. There is a separate set of procedures for that eventuality, which we covered earlier.

UNDERSTANDING "LOCAL RULES"

Every golf course is different in some way or another and it is for this reason that Local Rules were introduced in the first place. They are designed to take into account, and legislate for, the unique and varying conditions and circumstances that exist at courses around the country. They are not intended to override, or rewrite, the Rule Book.

Often these Local Rules are printed on the back of the score card and in virtually all cases there should be an appropriate list of the local rules posted on the notice board in the clubhouse. If you are visiting a course for the first time, or indeed if you're an established member but have never taken the trouble to check out the Local Rules, make yourself aware of them before your next round. Remember, these rules relate specifically to the course you are playing so they inevitably come into play on a regular basis. For that reason they are every bit as significant as the Rules of Golf themselves. The penalties are every bit as real, too.

Out of bounds These areas are usually marked by white stakes or lines, but sometimes it isn't as obvious as that. Remember the definition for out of bounds—it relates to areas on which *play is not permitted*. But they won't always be marked. An example might be, say, a row of flowerbeds between the

> " All greens are aerated at least once a year, sometimes twice, and for a short period of time afterward it can create problems for golfers. The turf-and-soil "plugs" that are removed from the green obviously leave unsightly holes. But not only are these unsightly, they are also problematical because a ball can nestle in one of the holes, making it difficult for a player to hit a smoothly-rolling putt. In such circumstances a committee will often introduce a Local Rule allowing golfers to mark and replace a ball to the side of an aeration hole. Like all Local Rules, it's in your interest to know about it. "

clubhouse and the back of the 18th green. If your ball finishes here you might simply think of it as a tough lie, or at worst an unplayable lie, but that might not be the case. It could well be out of bounds, which means if you proceed under the wrong rule and don't rectify your actions immediately, you are disqualified.

If cables are a regular feature at a course then a Local Rule will permit relief from such a condition.

Unusual obstructions

Most obstructions are clearly accounted for in the rule book, but some might catch you out. Local Rules exist to help you avoid such misinterpretation. Common examples might be, say, a flag-pole, a sleeper-wall around a green, white posts or chains surrounding a teeing area. These objects should all be provided for under the Local Rules to allow golfers to follow the correct procedures. You would usually get a drop from such things if they interfered with your stance or your swing, but don't expect a free drop just because they obscure your line of play. Another example might be overhead power lines crossing a fairway. A Local Rule could exist that allows a golfer to replay a shot if the ball hits these power lines.

Roads on the course Remember, the purpose of Local Rules is to classify certain areas or objects on the course that might otherwise provide confusion. A classic example of this would be the road on the 17th hole of the Old Course at St Andrews. Anyone who is familiar with this historic course will appreciate the fascination of the hole. At most golf clubs you would almost certainly be entitled to a free drop from an artificially covered path such as this, but not at St Andrews. Quite rightly, they believe that providing relief off the road would completely ruin the character, charm and degree of difficulty of the 17th. It would become a less fearsome hole—quirky but devoid of much of its challenge and appeal. So, anyone finishing on the road has to play the ball as it lies. No other road or path is likely to

■ *The road behind the 17th green at St Andrews is one of the few artificially-covered paths that golfers are obliged to play from.*

be as famous as this one, though, so unless you're on the Old Course you'd better check out the Local Rules.

Drop zones These are very easily missed if you're not alert. They mostly exist around putting surfaces, often when large areas of turf are subject to ground under repair making it impractical to follow certain relief options. Drop zones are usually sensibly positioned, not only making them easy to see but also representing an equitable solution for affected golfers. It certainly wouldn't be fair to put a drop zone in a position where you had to pitch over a bunker, when the ground under repair from which you've just plucked your ball was in nothing like as tricky a spot. Do always be on the lookout for them, though, because they might not always be conspicuous.

■ *At the start of every season young professionals are given a lecture on the nuances of the Rules of Golf.*

Young trees and plants Obviously it would be insane to spend a fortune on planting young trees, only to then let hoards of visiting golfers go marching into the planted area. The Greens Committee will rightly designate these areas as ground under repair, thus allowing you a free drop out of the newly-planted zone. This is one of the rare instances on a golf course where the rules conspire to put you in a genuinely more favorable position than before, as you drop from probably a quite wayward position back toward the line of

play. Which is good news for you, but even better news for the saplings. Any young tree that is staked should be dropped away from, without penalty.

Plugged balls This is one example of a Local Rule touched on earlier. On closely mown areas, such as fairways or walkways cut through rough, you are always entitled to relief from a ball plugged in its own

pitch-mark. In the winter, though, many clubs will extend this rule to include plugged balls in the rough as well. The only difference is that on the fairway you are allowed to clean your ball, whereas in the rough you will not be afforded that privilege.

Preferred lies This refers to a committee decision also known as "winter rules." That terminology gives the game away somewhat. It relates to the time of year when golf courses are not at their best; a time when greens committees grant concessions to all weather-beaten, possibly frostbitten, golfers. Basically the rule states that any time your ball is on the fairway, you are allowed to place it within six inches of where the ball originally came to rest. Just make sure you stick a tee-peg in the ground to mark the position of the ball before you move it.

This is all very handy if you don't much like the look of your lie, or if the ball is caked in mud. However, try not to get into the habit of automatically taking a preferred lie unless it's really necessary, otherwise you'll possibly find it a bit of a shock when spring comes around. On the whole, though, this rule is sensible and welcome. Not only can you encounter some frightful lies in the fairway during winter, but it is also felt that preferred lies help protect the course from unnecessary damage.

RULES Q & A

Learn by example may be an over-used phrase, but it's usually true nonetheless. So in time-honored tradition, let's look at a few examples of the rules constructed in a question and answer format. To avoid confusion, names have been attached to the imaginary participants in this eventful, and blunder-full round of golf.

Flagstick *faux pas*

Q Fred is on the green, facing a 40-foot putt. Being eagle-eyed and aggressive by nature, he has the flag taken out. Unfortunately his fellow competitor, a vacant youngster by the name of Ian, leaves the flag only a few yards from the hole. Fred is focused on the putt, he doesn't spot the potential dangers awaiting him and strokes the ball toward the hole. But it's too firm—a bit on the wide side, too—and Fred's ball collides with the flagstick. What's the outcome?

A Fred's glum expression gives the game away. He's on the green and his ball has struck the flagstick, so it's a two-stroke penalty. The only upside for Fred is that he can play the ball as it lies, which is nearer to the hole than it would have been if the flag hadn't been there. Small consolation, though, and he wouldn't even have that crumb of comfort in match play, because this offense carries a penalty of loss of hole.

Moving balls

Q Dave is in the rough. It's not uncommon, but this is unusual even for Dave because the ball has somehow become perched up in thick grass, several inches above the ground. Unperturbed, Dave gets ready to address the ball and, just as he is about to do so, the ball topples off its perch and comes to rest between his feet. Now Dave's confused. What does he do next?

A That's no problem for Dave. Strictly speaking he hasn't addressed the ball until he has grounded the club behind the ball—that rule doesn't apply in bunkers and other hazards, though. So it's no penalty. If Dave had grounded the club, he would have been deemed to have addressed the ball and if it moved after that point, it would be a one stroke penalty and the ball would have to be replaced on its original spot.

Change of heart

Q Vic has been known to be a bit shaky on the short putts, but things are going well in the final of the summer knockout. He's all-square with two to play and, on the 17th green, nudges a long putt to within a couple of feet of the hole. Mike, his opponent in this final, is at the opposite end of the green and, thinking the putt is stone-dead, concedes Vic's putt. But just as Vic is about to pick it up, Mike realizes the ball isn't that close after all and changes his mind. "Actually, you can't have that," says Mike, "it's a bit further away than I thought." Can Vic pick it up anyway?

A Indeed Vic can. A concession cannot be withdrawn—neither can it be refused. It's just tough that Mike forgot Vic was shaky on the shorties—and it's his own fault that he failed to spot how far away the ball was from the hole. Vic went on to win the match and Mike won't be so hasty next time he thinks about conceding a crucial putt.

Bunker blues

Q Alan's a bit of a wiz in the sand and, faced with a pretty daunting downhill lie, steps into the bunker confident of making good his escape and saving par on this tough par-3. "Hell," thinks Alan to himself, "I've holed shots a lot tougher than this." Things don't go according to plan, however. The slope is severe and the clubhead touches the sand in the backswing. It throws Alan's rhythm completely and he thins the ball into the face of the bunker, leaving him not with the anticipated par putt, but instead another bunker shot. But what's the ruling about touching the sand in the backswing?

A It's not good news for Alan. He is penalized for touching the sand before making his stroke. If you recall the definition of the word *stroke,* it states that it is "the forward momentum of the club made with the intention of fairly striking at and moving the ball." Well, Alan's swing hadn't got to the "forward momentum" part, so he is penalized in the same way as he would be if the clubhead had touched the sand at address. Harsh as it seems, it's a two-shot penalty for Alan. Being the unflappable type, Alan at least holes his next bunker shot—even though it is for a five.

Early morning call

Q It's a damp, autumn morning. Trevor marks his ball on the first green and taps it down with his trusty putter. Horror of horrors, the coin that Trevor uses to mark his ball sticks to the sole of his putter due to the dampness of the greens. Trevor is a bit slow to react and before he can recover the situation the coin falls off the sole of his putter and on to the green about five feet away from its original spot. The penny has finally dropped…literally, but what does Trevor do next?

A Trevor is in for a pleasant surprise. Since the coin moved in the process of him marking the ball, there is no penalty. Naturally, he must try to identify as accurately as possible where the marker was originally placed and put it back on that spot. Other than that he can proceed as normal.

Wrong side of the fence

Q Pete hooks his drive perilously close to the out-of-bounds fence on the 15th and, being the conscientious type, takes out a 3-iron for safety and plays a provisional ball into the middle of the fairway. Pete's fellow competitor, Phil, walks on ahead and, on reaching the out-of-bounds fence, yells back to Pete that he's found his first ball. It's in bounds after all. Pete picks up his provisional ball and marches forward only to discover that the ball by the fence isn't his ball at all. Pete then discovers that his ball is, in fact, out of bounds. What does he do next?

A It's not Pete's fault, but alas he gets hit for a one-stroke penalty. Why? Because he's moved what had become the "ball in play," without the authority to do so. Pete must then replace the provisional ball where it came to rest which, looking on the bright side, is at least on the fairway. Phil had better not expect a drink from Pete at the 19th.

Who's next up?

Q Mark and Alan are playing in the final of the winter foursomes knockout. Things are getting tight and Mark slices his tee shot close to some bushes on the 12th. They decide to play a provisional ball, in effect the third shot on that hole, but are somewhat baffled as to which one of them should hit the shot.

A Alan should be the one to play the provisional ball. Always bear in mind that penalty strokes do not affect the order of play, so even though the usual order in foursomes would require Mark to hit the third shot on a hole if he had teed-off, that isn't the case with a provisional ball.

Hot temper can be costly

Q Steve has been known to lose his cool on the golf course. He's better than he used to be as a youngster, but in the wrong situation you can almost see the blood boiling just below his calm exterior. This is one of those situations. Trying to escape from a nasty lie in the bunker to the side of the 6th green, he takes too much sand and leaves the ball in the bunker. That's enough to trigger Steve off—he slams his club in anger deep into the sand, and takes a kick at some sand just for good measure. Jonathan, his fellow competitor, is worried—not because Steve has lost his temper, but because he suspects a rules infringement has occurred. Is he right?

A Indeed he is. Jonathan has rightly identified that Steve's actions are in breach of rule 13, which prevents a player from touching the sand with the club. That's a two-stroke penalty for poor Steve. But it's just as bad for Jonathan—he has to pluck up the courage to break the news to him!

Mister casual

Q Mark is a casual sort of player, hardly ever taking the game too seriously. So when he rolls a long putt virtually stone-dead, he picks up the flagstick on his way to the hole and, with the flag still in his left hand and his putter in the right hand, nonchalantly taps the ball in. Has Mark broken any rule?

A No. As long as the ball doesn't strike the flag there is nothing wrong with doing this, except to say you can look a complete idiot if you miss.

STRANGE BUT TRUE

Golf can be a funny old game. Not just funny hah, hah, either, but funny strange, too. Indeed, the game's capacity for producing bizarre on-course scenarios really is quite astonishing. Incidents that might be considered rare, or perhaps even inconceivable, do happen to ordinary golfers like you and me.

Here are a few examples that slot nicely into the strange-but-true category. They might not happen to you...but you never know. They will help you appreciate how a simple understanding of the rules can resolve the strangest incidents imaginable.

Stroke-and-distance, thank you very much A player hits a full-blooded iron shot which hits a tree-stump and bounces back fully 60 yards behind him, landing right in the middle of a bush. It's now totally unplayable. Of course one of the options in an unplayable lie is stroke-and-distance, which means adding a stroke to the score and going back to the spot where the last shot was played. But in this case that option would involve going forward 60 yards nearer the hole. Surely that can't be allowed. Well, actually it can. Even though the player is in effect gaining 60 yards, stroke-and-distance means just what it says, even if as is the case here the distance happens to be of the forward variety.

Sit on the fence A player's ball comes to rest against a wire mesh out-of-bounds fence behind a green, making it impossible even to rest the clubhead behind the ball, let alone make a backswing. This is an ingenious golfer, though. He grabs his 9-iron and climbs over the fence. So he's now out of bounds. He then takes up his address position, with the fence between the clubface and the ball, takes an almighty swing and hits the fence, causing the ball to hop forward on to the green, only a few feet from the flag. If his 9-iron survived the experience, it would be amazing enough. But even more amazing is the fact that the player did nothing wrong. Anyone is entitled to stand out of bounds to play a ball that lies in bounds. And since the ball was fairly struck at, admittedly with a fence in the way, the stroke is allowed.

Ace...or no ace? On a totally blind par-3, a golfer knocks his tee shot over the hill and proceeds on to the green where a ball is lying 25 feet from the hole. Not a bad result, he thinks. But...oh dear. He putts up toward the hole and, as he goes to tap the ball in, sees his original ball lying in the hole.

■ The "Bunkered Pike" was found washed up on the 11th. fairway of Ireland's Hermitage Golf Course in 1939. The fish had a large bed-spring embedded in its lower jaw!

A hole-in-one! But his first thought is one of horror—surely he is penalized for playing the wrong ball. Actually, no he isn't. A hole is completed when the ball in play comes to rest in the hole, so the ace stands.

Bad arithmetic Two players leave the 18th green after a match play competition, one thinking the other has won. It's only when they are in the bar discussing the details of the match that they both realize the match was all-square after 18. Fortunately, there's a member of the committee in the bar at the time. They ask him if they can down their pints and head off to the first tee for a sudden-death playoff. No they can't. The match result stands, because there is no indication that any wrong information was given or received.

Guided missile A player really winds himself up for a big drive, but in the flurry of movement that passes as his downswing, the clubhead snaps away from the shaft. The player can't stop himself and still swings at the ball, but misses it. The clubhead doesn't miss, though, rebounding off the turf and deflecting the ball a few yards off its tee peg. Is there a penalty? No there isn't. The player attempted to make a stroke, fair and square. It was just unfortunate that the clubhead snapped off. He must compose himself and play the ball as it lies.

INDEX/CROSS REFERENCE
GUIDE